Willa Kim

Willa Kim, c. 1967. Courtesy of Willa Kim. Photo by Jack Mitchell.

WILLA ✦ KIM

written by
Bobbi
Owen

foreword by
Tony
Walton

The Designs of Willa Kim / by Bobbi Owen
ISBN: 1-933348-00-3

Series editor: Delbert Unruh
Editing services: Lynn Roundtree
Book design: Deborah Hazlett
Published in conjunction with
  Broadway Press
  David Rodger, publisher

First printing February 2005
Manufactured in the United States of America

United States Institute for Theatre Technology, Inc.
6443 Ridings Rd., Syracuse NY 13206

800.938.7488
www.usitt.org

Contents

Willa Kim, 1971. Courtesy of Willa Kim.

Foreword

For so many of us in this challenging field, Willa is not only an icon but the ultimate role model. A creature of limitless elegance and grace who paints and draws like a dream and is a relentless and entirely admirable perfectionist. Michael Smuin, who choreographed *Dancin' with Gershwin*, the Gershwin ballet that Willa designed for him in May 2001, told me that, having done so much work with Willa over the years, he was expecting her to be slowing down a bit by now. But as it turned out, she worked longer hours—and with more attention to detail—than anyone else on the project. "Slowing down?" said Michael, "Willa? Fat chance!"

Speaking of elegance and grace, my wife, Gen, once borrowed a beautiful cape from Willa that almost led to Gen's only act of larceny! To be wearing something of Willa Kim's made her entirely euphoric. In fact, Gen mentioned that, if it came down to it, she'd even be happy to wear a thumb tack that had been hammered into her head by Willa.

Alongside Willa the incomparable artist and the soul of grace is Willa the wondrously wacky chum who can stay out cavorting until at least 4 a.m.—as she did with William Ivey Long, whooping it up after the 2001 Tony Awards.

Willa is always the life of the party and the last to head bedwards. As hungry for life as she often seems to be for her next meal—and the next one! (And what a perfectionist she is, too, as a dinner companion. It is thrilling to observe her selecting, in microscopic detail, just exactly what she's hungry for *and* how it should be presented.)

I was first conscious of seeing Willa's amazing design work (and being dumfounded by it) over thirty years ago with her costumes for Jean Genet's *The Screens*, and I have become increasingly in awe of her in the course of all the productions we have worked on together over the past twenty years or so.

I often find myself regretting that these days I seldom design both the sets and the costumes for shows, as I used to do in my earlier years. But I never feel this when working with Willa. I *know* I could never come *close* to the glories she is able to produce.

Our many collaborations over the past years include innumerable ballets, four or more straight plays, at least three big Broadway musicals, and *Tosca* twice (for San Francisco and for Chicago).

For our *Tosca* (costume designer legend has it) Willa even exceeded her usual level of perfectionism by designing a stunning costume for Scarpia for the third act—*after* he is dead!

The unexpected "extra" may well have been the result of her strong mystical streak, which also sometimes leads her to leave mysterious phone messages, such as, "Call me. I'm… …Well…I don't actually know where I am!"

But of course she does. She's at the top of the pile—the head of the class—the pinnacle of success—the winning post. As she is with every overwhelmingly deserved Lifetime Achievement Award* she receives.

But what lifetime? Is it *another* lifetime already? She had one lifetime honored only a few years ago when she won the Irene Sharaff Award [1999]. But Willa has such an abundance of energy, enthusiasm, free-flowing genius, and stick-to-itiveness that to me, it seems certain that she has at least two more lifetimes of extraordinary work and achievement ahead of her!

So let's congratulate—and toast—her as we look forward to reveling in the glory of all that!

Bravo, Willa! Like everyone you've ever met, I love you.

Tony Walton

* The preceding text was adapted from Tony Walton's presentation speech when the League of Professional Theatre Women awarded the Ruth Morley Designing Woman Award to Willa Kim on June 7, 2001. Tony Walton began by saying how honored he was to be presenting the award to the wondrous Willa Kim as a prestigious addition to the Tonys, Emmys, Drama Desks, and so forth she had already received. Since then she has been given a Lifetime Achievement Award from the Fashion Institute of Technology, and coinciding with the publication of this book, she is being given the USITT Distinguished Achievement Award in Costume Design. -ed.

Preface

I first met Willa Kim in 1986 when I was doing the illustrations for my first book, Costume Design on Broadway (Greenwood Press, 1987). To say that I was surprised when she invited me to her Upper West Side apartment would be an understatement. She was busy with many projects and in great demand, having just received a Tony Award nomination for Song & Dance. As we sat and talked in her lovely living room, I was concerned about spilling tea on her gorgeous oriental rug and turning the delicate cookies she had served me into crumbs, but she made me feel so welcome that I soon stopped worrying and began enjoying the opportunity to talk with her. Before our meeting I had been a fan of her designs; since that day I've become fond of her as a person as well.

They say it takes enthusiasm for a subject to be able to write well—and if this book is at fault in any way, it's not because Willa Kim hasn't inspired me. She has been wonderful, and I hope this volume adequately represents my admiration for her artistry. This book is based on a series of visits with her in New York over the last twenty years—though nothing so formal as an interview has ever occurred. Our conversations have taken place in a variety of settings: over dinner in several restaurants, during walks arm-in-arm down Broadway, and at her apartment while nibbling on apple strudel from Zabar's, surrounded by her art and her research materials. I have even bombarded her with questions while leaning over the counter in her kitchen as she prepared tea in one of her heirloom Korean tea pots.

We get along—and not just because she's a Cancer and I'm a Virgo. We share a love of research, of theatre and dance, and of costume design. And we both admire the artistic quality in a painting or drawing created with a few well-placed lines and a splash of color.

I owe a deep debt of gratitude to a number of people who helped make this book possible: Lynn Roundtree, who edited the text, and who has provided excellent advice and assistance with all my books; David Rodger, who always finds ways to support writers interested in entertainment design and technology; Del Unruh, editor of the United States Institute for Theatre Technology's new monograph series, for whom this book represents an old dream realized; the wonderful Deborah Hazlett for the beautiful design she has created for this book; the members of the Publications Committee and the Board of Directors of USITT, in particular Bruce Brockman, who was president when this idea for a series of monographs about major American designers was first mentioned; Judy Adamson and Brian Russman, for phone numbers, contacts, willingness to listen to my stories and anecdotes about costume designers, many meals, and much hospitality; and most of all my husband, Gordon Ferguson, the love of my life, who works wonders with databases and computers and who always supports my many activities. It is also important to express my appreciation to USITT. The Institute supports and advocates for its members in the field of entertainment design and offers many ways to be active—and rewards for those who are.

At the University of North Carolina at Chapel Hill, I have benefited from support from the Department of Dramatic Art, the College of Arts and Sciences (and its Fund for Scholarly Activities), the Institute for the Arts and Humanities (where I have been a Summer Fellow, a Chapman Family Faculty Fellow, and a Leadership Fellow), the Center for Teaching and Learning, and from two semester-long Pogue research fellowships. The UNC Library is a wonderful asset, and much of what I do would not be possible without the resources it provides, in print, on microfilm, and in electronic form.

It has long been my dream to write a book about a small group of great American costume designers who, in my opinion, either founded or through their artistry made costume design a noteworthy specialization. In the course of my research, I found myself having to write four books to understand the development of the profession of costume design in America. I didn't know then that I would need to write a whole series of books instead of just one about the "costume designers who shook the world." Willa Kim was on that original list in 1985, as were Theoni V. Aldredge, Lucinda Ballard, Will R. Barnes, Florence Klotz, Charles LeMaire, Raoul Pène du Bois, Irene Sharaff, Caroline Siedle, and Patricia Zipprodt. This book is dedicated to them all.

One down, nine to go!

Bobbi Owen
January 2005
Chapel Hill, NC

Introduction

If I'm doing a ballet, I want to see the movements of each dancer before I begin.
Willa Kim

Walking the halls and costume workrooms at Paramount Studios was one way for Willa Kim to feel busy. She had been doing fashion illustration in Los Angeles for the May Company but gave it up to join Paramount. A month later there was little to do, what designs she saw were uninspired, and no one she met was particularly interesting. *Why have I come here,* she wondered.

A portfolio poised carefully on a desk captured her attention as she wandered among the costume workrooms, offices, and fitting rooms. She boldly went into the office and opened it. What she found stunned her and the lifeless film factory was suddenly transformed into a place of beauty and wonder. The office was Karinska's and the sketches, by Raoul Pène du Bois, were for *Lady in the Dark*. Miss Kim did not yet know of their reputations, but she responded immediately to their artistry. And they responded to hers. Paramount had been a brilliant choice.

In the early 1950s she relocated to New York and assisted Raoul Pène du Bois on some of the great Broadway musicals of that era: *Wonderful Town, Bells Are Ringing, The Music Man,* and *Gypsy.*

When *Red Eye of Love* opened in New York in 1961 Willa Kim's career as a theatrical designer really began. From Adrienne Kennedy's ground-breaking play about race relations, *Funnyhouse of a Negro* (1964), to Robert Lowell's *The Old Glory* she chose projects she admired—and found theatrical. For *The Old Glory*, Willa Kim received the first of her many awards for costume design, the 1964-1965 Obie Award for outstanding costume design.

Her reputation grew quickly. She designed more off-Broadway plays, her first opera (*The Stag King* for the Santa Fe Opera) and soon afterwards her first Broadway show, Edward Albee's *Malcolm* in 1966.

At their debut at the New York City Center of Music and Drama in 1966, the Joffrey Ballet premiered *Nightwings*, choreographed by Gerald Arpino, and performed a revised version of Robert Joffrey's *Gamelan*. Both ballets featured costumes by Willa Kim, and some of her signature design elements: "a whiff of period" and "a suggestion of place."

The year 1968 saw Willa Kim's triumphant return to the Santa Fe Opera Company for a new production of *The Magic Flute*. She also continued to design for dance and plays, including *Operation Sidewinder* by Sam Shepard, which opened on March 12, 1970. Willa Kim's insistence on reproducing her costume designs exactly as they were shown on her sketches, in particular for the character "Honey," led her to create an entirely new way of painting and dyeing costumes, which has become the industry standard. *Operation Sidewinder* also marked the beginning of another of Willa Kim's signature design elements: custom-painted costumes.

Her innovation would soon transform dance costumes. In 1971 Studio co-founder Betty Williams, asked Willa Kim to consider some new fabric—Lycra Spandex—for the designs for Margo Sappington's *Weewis*. When the costumes were made and the garments painted with dyes in the exact colors that Willa Kim had specified, the results were remarkable. Two years later, Miss Kim designed *Remembrances* for Robert Joffrey. Sally Ann Parsons, who was then at Ray Diffen's Studio, made the *Remembrances* costumes out of the same stretchy fabric. The revolution had begun.

Legs Diamond
Costume Rendering by Willa Kim for Carol Ann Baxter (SK# 180), Deanna Dys (SK# 182), and Colleen Dunn (SK# 183) for the Funeral Scene, 1988. Courtesy of Willa Kim.

Soon after the opening of *Weewis*, Willa Kim designed costumes for the American premiere of Jean Genet's *The Screens*, for which she won several awards, including the 1972 Drama Desk Award. During her first ten years in the business, she had designed costumes for some fifty plays and ballets, and her reputation as a designer of wit and intelligence was established.

From 1963 and 1976 Willa Kim had her "Joffrey Years," with her designs appearing in several ballets including *Gamelan* (1963), *Game of Noah* (1965), *Nightwings* (1966), *Weewis* (1971), *Jive* (1973), *Tactics* (1976), *Orpheus Times Light Squared* (1976), and *Face Dancers* (1976).

Jive was especially important, because it was the first ballet she designed for Eliot Feld, with whom she would ultimately collaborate on more than sixty pieces. Even as she began designing for Eliot Feld (leading to her "Feld Years"), she continued to design for other choreographers, including Glen Tetley and Michael Smuin.

This affinity for dance extended to her most successful Broadway productions, which have mainly been dance-based. When *Goodtime Charley* opened on Broadway in 1975, Willa Kim received the first of her six Tony Award nominations for the costumes. Her second came in 1978, with *Dancin'*.

Early in 1980, Willa Kim designed a full-length ballet, *The Tempest*, for the San Francisco Ballet, choreographed by Michael Smuin. It opened to rave reviews, and she received her first Emmy Award when it was broadcast on the *Dance in America* series. The following year, Willa Kim won a Tony Award for her wonderful costumes for *Sophisticated Ladies*. Her next Broadway production, *Song & Dance*, opened on September 18, 1985, and for her designs she received her fourth Tony Award nomination. Her fifth would occur with *Legs Diamond*.

In the mid-1980s she designed two full-length plays, Eugene O'Neill's *Long Day's Journey into Night,* and *The Front Page* by Ben Hecht and Charles MacArthur. Each presented exciting opportunities to develop character within long pieces (rather than the shorter format ballets she had been doing). Between them she continued to design new dances by Eliot Feld.

Willa Kim received her sixth Tony Award nomination—and second Tony Award—for *The Will Rogers Follies* in 1991. The very successful Broadway show was the first of a series of musicals she would do with Tommy Tune: *Tommy Tune Tonite!, Grease,* and *Stage Door Charley.* By 1995 all three shows were touring throughout the United States. Meanwhile Miss Kim was busy in New York overseeing the construction of her costume designs for a new Broadway musical starring Julie Andrews, *Victor/Victoria.*

As she started to be the recipient of career achievement awards, someone asked Miss Kim if she might be considering retiring. The response was an adamant "no," followed by a list of her current projects and a paean to the joy she continued to find while designing.

When Willa Kim was awarded the 1999 TDF/Irene Sharaff Lifetime Achievement Award from the Theatre Development Fund, she was busy designing new ballets for Eliot Feld and Michael Smuin and new plays by Maria Irene Fornés and Gen LeRoy.

When Miss Kim received The Ruth Morley Designing Woman Award from The League of Professional Theatre Women in 2001, she was busy doing shows at the Bay Street Theatre in Sag Harbor, the Williamstown Theatre Festival, and the Stamford Center for the Arts.

When she received the Fashion Institute of Technology's 2003 Patricia Zipprodt Award for Innovative Costume Design in 2003, she was designing *Havana under the Sea* off-Broadway, *An Enemy of the People* at the Williamstown Theatre Festival, and *St. Louis Woman* for The Dance Theatre of Harlem.

When the announcement was made that Willa Kim would receive the 2005 Distinguished Achievement Award in Costume Design from the United States Institute for Theatre Technology, she had just completed designs for *The Bay at Nice* at Hartford Stage and *The Immigrant* at Dodger Stages. She was also busy designing a new production of *Turandot* for the Santa Fe Opera, scheduled to open on July 1, 2005.

Miss Kim already ranks among the most distinguished American costume designers, but her achievements are not yet finished. As any of her many friends and admirers will readily testify, she continues to seek "interesting projects."

A Footstep of Air
Costume Design by Willa Kim for Edmund LaFosse and Megan Murphy, 1977.
Choreography by Eliot Feld for The Feld Ballet. Courtesy of Willa Kim. Photo © Lois Greenfield.

Part One • The Early Years

Willa Kim was born Wullah Mei Ok (Oak) Kim near Santa Ana, California, and moved to Los Angeles by age one. As in many traditional Korean families her parents' marriage was arranged when they were very young. Her father, Shoon Kwan Kim, had immigrated with a cousin to the United States in 1905 from Inchon, Korea, where the family business, recovering salt from seawater, had been affected by the Japanese declaration of a protectorate that year. Laboring in a variety of farming-related jobs on the West Coast they moved gradually south, from Seattle to Southern California.

Shoon Kwan Kim left his cousin in Reedley, California and moved closer to Los Angeles, where he worked as a farm laborer and fruit stand vendor and attended night school to learn English. Throughout his life, he remained interested in Korean politics, mainly through the nationalist movement of Syngman Rhee (1875-1965). Rhee, a strong voice for Korean independence, was head of the Korean government in exile and in 1948 became the first president of the Republic of Korea. Rhee had strong support from the Korean community in the United States, including from Willa Kim's father, who was an active fund-raiser for the nationalists.

Willa Kim's mother, Nora (Nora Koh) Kim immigrated to the United States in 1916. She was raised in a farming family near Suwon, Korea, and graduated from Ewha Woman's University in Seoul. (Ewha Haktang, founded by the Women's Foreign Missionary Society of the Methodist Episcopal Church, had been established in 1886.) With the assistance of the missionaries at the university, Nora came to the U.S. intending to study theology in Chicago, but when she arrived in Seattle, the United States Custom Service officials notified her husband, because she was legally married. Without his permission, she could not travel to Chicago or attend school. Instead of going to school she was sent to Shoon Kwan Kim in California, and soon found herself the mother of small children and proprietor of a grocery story at the corner of Temple and Flower Streets in Los Angeles (near the site of the current Los Angeles Music Center).

Willa and her brother, Young Oak, had as much of a traditional Korean upbringing as was possible in the relatively small Korean community in Los Angeles, attending Korean school in the afternoon after classes at their local public school. Her sister, Mary Ko, and her younger brothers Jack, Philip, and Henry, were more assimilated into American culture, even as Shoon Kwan became more involved in Korean politics. The Kim's ended up separating and Nora became responsible for running the grocery store, as well as rearing their six children.

Portfolio Sketches by Willa Kim, c. 1940. Courtesy of Willa Kim.

As early as grammar school and throughout her high school years at Los Angeles' Belmont High School, Willa Kim knew she would become an artist. Her younger brothers all showed some artistic ability, but their talent was not supported in the same way as Willa's was.

Encouraged to draw, she did so even in music class, only in part because she couldn't sing. Her grades were not especially strong, but she always received high marks for content even when she got low ones for spelling. She was encouraged by her teachers and was seen as a creative young woman who showed much promise. She was sought out for her ability to draw and even designed the end papers for the senior yearbook at Belmont High.

When she graduated from high school, Willa decided to become a fashion illustrator and a painter. She soon enrolled in art classes at Los Angeles City College where she studied with (among other classmates) Rudi Gernreich (1922–1985), an aspiring fashion designer. Miss Kim wore some of Gernreich's early designs and continued to do so for a number of years, as his own label grew and his career developed.

Willa Kim won a scholarship to attend the Chouinard Institute of Art in Los Angeles. Her classmates at Chouinard included Pauline Annon, the well-known Los Angeles-based fashion illustrator, and George Stave, the still-life and landscape painter. (Stave later married Margaret Stark, the widely collected abstract painter, one of Miss Kim's earliest friends in New York.)

Another Chouinard classmate was Tom Keogh (1921-1980), an artist, designer, and illustrator, with credits including the first cover of Paris *Vogue*. Willa Kim formed life-long friendships with Pauline Annon and Tom Keogh during their time at Chouinard. In and outside of the classroom, these talented friends inspired one another and helped each other develop their artistic talents.

Tom Keogh's artistic sensibility was especially important to Kim, in large part as a confirmation of her own artistic impulses. Intelligent, witty and gifted, Keogh introduced Kim to a Los Angeles social scene with which she was unfamiliar. His California-style sociability contrasted with her more conservative and reserved Korean upbringing.

Willa Kim admired the work of the fashion illustrators Eric (the pen name of Carl Erickson) and Dorothy Hood. Carl Oscar August Erickson (1891-1958) was one of the most influential illustrators of his generation. A regular contributor to *Vogue* from the eve of the First World War until after World War II, his fluid, impressionistic style—a few lines and a splash of color—was markedly different from that of his colleagues. Eric's drawings evidenced a freedom plus the elegance and style of a master draftsman.

Another influential fashion illustrator of the time was Dorothy Hood (1904-1970), creator of the "The Hood Girl" that became synonymous with the Lord & Taylor department store. Her watercolor-washed drawings of young, fashionable women were wildly successful during the 1930s and 1940s.

Completing her studies at Chouinard, she searched for a position as a commercial artist. One of her art instructors set up an interview with Al Nichols at Western Costume Company, who asked if he could keep her portfolio to show to colleagues in the movie business.

In October 1942, Willa Kim landed work at the May Company in Los Angeles as a fashion illustrator, which she considered to be her "dream job." At the May Company she worked in the art department on Broadway in a studio with several other sketch artists, often doing drawings of live models dressed in the company's fashions. While at the May Company she worked on illustrations that appeared in the *Los Angeles Times* in November of that year. One of these advertisements, a full-page ad for stockings, was so well received that the company awarded her with a bonus of several pairs of nylon stockings—a much prized gift during this period of war-time rationing.

But her dream career as a fashion illustrator would last only one month. Al Nichols had circulated her portfolio to his contacts at Paramount Studios where Mitchell Leisen, director, and occasional designer at Paramount Studios, and Frank Richardson, head of Paramount's wardrobe department, were impressed with what they saw. She was offered a position at Paramount at a salary of seventy-five dollars a week, nearly twice her salary of forty-one dollars a week at the May Company. On the advice of another sketch artist at May, that fashion illustration was "a dying art form" (because of the advent of fashion photography), she accepted Leisen's offer and by December 1942 was on the staff at Paramount Studios.

Her first few weeks at Paramount were, by her own admission, not very interesting. Most anyone would have thought that the movie studio, where dozens of motion pictures were being planned and filmed at the same time, would have been exciting for Miss Kim. But it turned out that she spent long days in her office in the middle of a very long hall in the wardrobe department, with Edith Head's office at one end and the studio's costume workrooms at the other. Mary Kay Dodson, one of the newer Paramount designers, and Madame Barbara Karinska, the preeminent costume maker known to everyone simply as "Karinska," also had offices along the hall, adjacent to a series of fitting rooms. Except for traffic into and out of the fitting rooms, there was little activity.

It wasn't until she met and was assigned to work with Karinska on *Lady in the Dark* that Willa Kim found anything of interest to do in the entire place, sound stages included. Karinska "discovered" Willa Kim because, bored and without much to do, Willa sneaked into Karinska's office and opened the portfolio lying on her desk. The case contained designs by Raoul Pène du Bois for *Lady in the Dark*. They were wonderful.

Willa's enthusiasm for the sketches made her an excellent assistant, and even though she had no idea who Karinska was, she did what she was asked to do simply to be involved with the creativity implicit in the sketches by Pène du Bois. Soon she was creating full-scale drawings of all of Raoul Pène du Bois's sketches for the movie, on which he was serving as both art director and costume designer. Translating Pène du Bois's sketches into full-scale drawings allowed her to use her training as an artist. Willa Kim was instrumental in deciding where all the mink pelts would be placed in the famous "mink-skirted" dress that Ginger Rogers wore in the film, which was made under Karinska's close supervision. Although Raoul Pène du Bois designed costumes for most of the film, the modern gowns for the movie were designed by Edith Head, Babs Wilomez, and Mitchell Leisen.

The May Company: Gift Leg-ary
  Full-page advertisement in *Los Angeles Times*, Sunday, November 23, 1942. Part I, p. 19.
  Courtesy of The May Department Stores Company.

During the making of *Lady in the Dark*, Miss Kim delivered samples of her decorative elements for the movie's gowns to the studio workroom, made color swatches and carried them to the sound studios for camera tests, and as she later said, "helped make the garments as beautiful as the sketches."

Once *Lady in the Dark* (1944) was completed, Raoul, Karinska, and Willa worked together on *Frenchman's Creek* (1944), starring Joan Fontaine and Basil Rathbone, and *Kitty* (1945), starring Ray Milland and Paulette Goddard. All three films were directed by Mitch Leisen, who had started his career in the movies as a costume designer, then became an art director before making the transition to director. He maintained a strong interest in all visual aspects of the films on which he worked, often contributing costume designs to them (in particular for leading ladies) throughout his career.

Although she continued to live at home, Willa soon accumulated enough money to afford a car. Until Karinska learned to drive (she terrorized the studio lot practicing), Willa functioned as a quasi-chauffeur, often taking Karinska to her Malibu beach house and to a variety of locations throughout Los Angeles and Hollywood. Karinska introduced her to many artists, including Eugene Berman, the Russian painter and designer, and Marcel Vertés. She also met George Balanchine when he visited California.

She also, finally, met Raoul Pène du Bois (1912-1985) in person just as 1942 was ending. Willa not only became his assistant for many Broadway productions but a life-long friend. They went to parties together in the "After Hours" locations popular in Los Angeles during the Second World War. Even as the war effort intensified on the West Coast, Los Angeles was an exciting place to be. Many of the mansions on Adams Street were too expensive to maintain as homes during war time and were converted into "After Hours" clubs, where musicians went to jam after their regular performances. They entertained soldiers and the many employees of the movie studios, from costume makers and scene painters to film stars. After working long days in the studios there were equally enjoyable long nights in the clubs.

Willa Kim's friends loved coming to see her at Paramount because of the glamour associated with the movies. There was lots of activity and the presence of movie stars made the studios even more interesting. She arranged for guest passes, and her friends flocked to the studio, especially Tom Keogh.

Even though she was busy and happily working with Raoul Pène du Bois and Karinska at Paramount, Willa Kim continued to believe that this was a brief interlude and that her career as an artist and fashion illustrator would develop. One day when the workrooms were quiet, she carried her portfolio of drawings to Metro-Goldwyn-Mayer to show to the great movie designer, Irene (Irene Lentz, 1901-1962), who had been recently appointed Executive Designer by Louis B. Mayer. She sat in the reception area for a short time with another woman who was also waiting for Irene. When Tom Keogh came to meet her and take her to lunch, he told Willa that she had been sitting next to Marlene Dietrich.

Willa introduced Tom Keogh to Karinska who hired him as an assistant in 1943, and he worked with her on Dietrich's costumes for *Kismet*. When Karinska finally stopped commuting from coast to coast to supervise a variety of projects and settled once again in New York City, Tom followed her there and ultimately convinced Willa to relocate as well. Tom Keogh's ability as a sketch artist readily developed into design ability, and later he did the ballet sequence in the movie *Daddy Longlegs* (1954). He spent much of his career in Paris, making his name as a fashion illustrator for Paris *Vogue* and other French fashion magazines. He also designed ballets and illustrated many books, including those by his wife, Theodora Roosevelt Keogh.

In 1945, Willa Kim made her first trip to New York City, traveling by train across the country, to assist Raoul Pène du Bois on Broadway. The musical *Are You With It?*, starring Joan Roberts, Johnny Downs, Lew Parker, and Dolores Gray opened at the Century Theatre on November 10, 1945. It was the first of many Broadway musicals on which Miss Kim assisted Pène du Bois. A review two days later in the *New York Times* (November 12, 1945) was the first of many positive ones she would receive, saying that "being about a carnival, it has what a good carnival ought to have—colorful costumes by Willa Kim from sketches by Raoul Pène du Bois."

A few months later, she was credited with the costume designs for *The Duchess Misbehaves*. The musical comedy, set in eighteenth century Spain (after a short introductory scene in the art department of a modern department store), was delegated to her by Raoul Pène du Bois who was busy with designs for other productions. It opened on February 13, 1946, at the Adelphi Theatre, and starred Joey Faye as the painter Goya, with Audrey Christie and Paula Laurence, as leading ladies.

Housing in New York City was difficult to find in the mid-1940s, and both Tom and Willa were lucky to find dancers willing to share accommodations. Among their close associates were dancers Yevgeni (Simon) Semenov, who danced with the Marquis de Cuevas troupe and the Greek dancer Alexandros Iolas (1908-1987). One of Iolas' favorite dancing partners in the night clubs was Theodora Roosevelt, and it was through him that Tom Keogh met his future wife.

Through Karinska, Willa Kim also met Salvador Dali and other fine art painters who occasionally designed for the theatre. They invariably wanted Karinska to realize their designs, and Willa was part of that creation. For a ballet Dali designed for Russian–American dancer Andre Eglevsky (1917–77), Willa Kim became the envy of all her friends when she planned where the decorative jewels would go on Eglevsky's costume, while the dancer wore the unfinished garment. The ballet, *Sentimental Colloquy*, premiered in 1944. Willa Kim did not sew garments, or dye fabrics, or participate in any other facet of costume construction. As she has said, "I only did the art things."

After working with Raoul Pène du Bois on a couple more productions, Willa Kim returned to California to study at the Jepson Art Institute with the Italian painter and designer Rico Lebrun (1900-1964). He had been in the United States since the mid-1920s creating stained glass, murals, and commercial advertising mainly in Chicago and New York City, but he moved to southern California after World War II ended. After teaching for a short time at Chouinard, he worked with the animators at Disney Studios on *Bambi*. From 1947 until 1950 he taught at the Jepson Art Institute and was an especially popular teacher.

Willa Kim's brother, Young Oak Kim, returned to Los Angeles at about the same time Willa arrived back from New York City. A career military officer, he achieved the rank of colonel in the U.S. Army, and ended World War II a much-decorated hero, having received the only Congressional Medal of Honor presented to an Asian-American during the war.

When Willa Kim returned to New York early in 1950 to work once again with Raoul Pène du Bois, she moved into her own apartment at 107 West 46th Street in New York City. While she remained committed to being an artist and fashion illustrator, there were not many opportunities. She maintained studio space at Julian Marshall and Associates in Manhattan, an advertising agency, in exchange for occasional art work. Her primary focus, however, continued to be assisting Raoul Pène du Bois. Miss Kim became familiar with other costume construction houses, including Eaves Costume Company and Brooks Costume Company, because not all of the costumes for the productions Pène du Bois designed were made by Karinska. Through assisting Raoul Pène du Bois, she met many people associated with the dance and theatre, including Jerome Robbins, Jack Cole, Robin Gregory, and many others. Many of the dancers she associated with were beginning to do some choreography as well.

Raoul Pène du Bois designed *Alive and Kicking*, directed by Robert H. Gordon with choreography by Jack Cole, which opened at the Winter Garden Theatre on January 17,

1950, and *Call Me Madame*, with music and lyrics by Irving Berlin which opened on October 12 that same year. Jerome Robbins choreographed *Call Me Madame* and his work with dancers made a strong impression on Willa Kim, especially his attention to the way their bodies moved inside the costumes.

One of the dancers she met through Raoul Pène du Bois was Robin Gregory. Early in 1952, he convinced Willa Kim to do costumes for a production he was choreographing. It was to be done in contemporary clothes, and so appealed to the fashion illustrator in her. *The Rehearsal*, advertised as "A Restoration Comedy in Modern Dress," played only a few performances in May 1952. As the first-ever transfer from Equity Library Theatre to an off-Broadway house, it did, however, gain attention for some of the people associated with it, in particular Freda Miller and Van Williams, who wrote the songs. Walking down West 48th Street shortly before the show opened at the President Theatre, she was shocked to see her name on the marquee, in lights.

But soon, Willa Kim was again assisting Raoul Pène du Bois, on *Wonderful Town*, which opened on February 24, 1953. This was a big Broadway musicals with elaborate costumes that took many months to create. She was very busy, and by the time the production was open, Miss Kim needed a vacation.

In the fall of 1954, Willa Kim traveled to Europe with Margaret Stark, who was married to George Stave, one of Miss Kim's painter friends from Chouinard. These young artists had become friendly because they had each rented studio space on Second Avenue in New York, Willa's sublet from Larry Rivers. Stave had received a Fullbright Fellowship to travel in India,

The Student Gypsy, or *The Prince of Liedencrantz*
Costume Design by Raoul Pène du Bois, for two chorus dancers, 1963. Courtesy of Willa Kim. Photo by Jan Juracek.

leaving Margaret behind so she was free to tour through Spain and France with Miss Kim. Raoul Pène du Bois was in Paris, having gone there when his mother died. Willa and Margaret went to a party with Raoul Pène du Bois and met his cousins, William (Billy) Pène du Bois and his sister Yvonne Pène du Bois (later Yvonne McKenney). Willa and Margaret left for Spain the following day, and soon afterwards Margaret returned to the United States. Willa Kim, however, returned to Paris in time to attend a Thanksgiving Day party that Tom and Theodora Keogh were hosting for some American expatriates. Billy was at the party and they spent time together. The following day he took Willa around Paris, and showed her some of his favorite places, having lived there for many years. Her plans soon took her back to New York, but Billy followed her there. They were married in 1955, after his divorce from his first wife, Jane Michelle Bouché, became final.

William Sherman Pène du Bois (1916-1993) was the founding art director of the *Paris Review* and a widely published author and illustrator of popular children's books. Often using animals (in particular bears) as the lead characters in his stories, he won the American Library Association's John Newberry Medal for *The Twenty-One Balloons* in 1948, and two Caldecott Honor Awards. His book, *Bear Circus*, was named one of the Ten Best Children's Books in 1971 by the New York Times Book Review. Originally from Nutley, New Jersey, he spent much of his life in Paris, where he studied painting at the Lycée de Nice, the Lycée Hoche, and with his father, the artist Guy Pène du Bois. During service in the U.S. Army in World War II, he was a correspondent for *Yank* magazine.

When Raoul Pène du Bois also returned to New York he resumed working, with Willa Kim as his assistant, initially on *Mrs. Patterson*, which opened on December 1, 1954. The

Willa Kim and William Pène du Bois, c. 1968. Courtesy of
Willa Kim.

entire *Mrs. Patterson* production company, including Enid
Markey in the title role and Eartha Kitt in the leading role,
spent three weeks in Detroit and seven weeks in Chicago
before the show opened at the National Theatre on Broadway.

In the late 1950s Willa assisted Pène du Bois on some
of his largest and most successful Broadway musicals: *Bells
Are Ringing, The Music Man,* and *Gypsy* (for which he won
the Tony Award for costume design). She again observed
the connection between costumes and choreography
through the collaboration between Raoul Pène du Bois and
Jerome Robbins on *Gypsy.* She also met Bob Fosse for the
first time when he did some of the choreography for *Bells
Are Ringing* with Robbins. These were a busy few years, and
although Willa continued to pursue fashion illustration,
there were even fewer prospects.

After *Gypsy* opened, she and Billy returned to Europe,
this time sailing on an Italian ocean liner. They stopped in
Lisbon for a few days before disembarking, with their car, in
Sicily. From there they drove to Paris—the long way around,
taking several months. They toured the countryside, went
to museums, and visited friends along the way, including
Arnold Weinstein, who was working on a play while living
in Florence. All the while Willa was considering whether her
dream of being a fashion illustrator was realistic.

Back in New York in late 1960, Willa continued to feel
unsettled and unsure of what to do. As a result, at the suggestion of a friend and on a lark, she went to see an astrologer. He told her not to make any big decisions but rather to wait, patiently, for a while
longer.

She took his advice, and a short time later Arnold Weinstein called to ask her to design
costumes for his newly completed play, *Red Eye of Love.* The Living Theatre space was available, John Wulp would direct, Sam Cohn and John Wulp would produce (with assistance
from Julia Miles, as Associate Producer), and they needed a costume designer. The experience she had gained through her long apprenticeship assisting Raoul Pène du Bois and
working in Karinska's atelier helped Willa admit to herself what all her friends, family members, and colleagues already knew—that she was a costume designer.

With the opening of *Red Eye of Love* on June 12, 1961, Willa Kim in fact began her own
career as a costume designer. She never looked back, nor ever wished again that she had
continued to pursue a career as a fashion illustrator. She always had been and would always
be a painter. But her medium would not be stretched canvas nor be complete when she

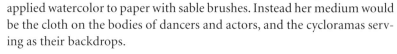

applied watercolor to paper with sable brushes. Instead her medium would
be the cloth on the bodies of dancers and actors, and the cycloramas serving as their backdrops.

Part Two • Becoming Established

Arnold Weinstein left messages for Willa Kim all around New York City at the beginning of 1961, before he was finally able to reach her by telephone to ask her to design costumes for *Red Eye of Love*. When the musical opened that summer at the Living Theatre not only was a new career born, Miss Kim was also introduced to a new set of artists who would soon become her colleagues and life-long collaborators.

During *Red Eye of Love* she met John Wulp, who designed the sets, directed, and was co-producer of the musical. The costume budget was not especially large (barely $250) but Willa found shopping for the costumes in mainstream stores and thrift shops to be an enjoyable experience. The production, about a department store selling nothing but meat as a parable for modern times, was a critical success when it opened on June 12, 1961, especially in the eyes of Walter Kerr, the influential critic who wrote for the *New York Herald Tribune*. It was also a success for Willa who got confirmation that her decision to become a costume designer was the correct one. Although the play did not garner very big audiences during the six-month run, the producers decided to do another production.

She would work with Weinstein on two additional productions, the comic opera *Dynamite Tonight!* which Weinstein wrote and co-directed with Paul Sills, and *Fortuna*, a musical version of a play by Eduardo de Filippo. Arnold Weinstein's adaptation of *Fortuna*, starring Jane Connell, opened at the Maidman Playhouse (later Playwrights Horizons) on January 3, 1963. The rehearsal schedule was exhausting and John Wulp, who was designing the sets as well as co-producing and directing, needed help. Choreographer Glen Tetley, initially hired to do some choreography, became a replacement director. While the play did not get very good reviews, the way in which Tetley moved the actors around the stage was applauded by the critics. And, perhaps most importantly, Willa Kim and Glen Tetley solidified a working relationship that would continue for decades—mainly in dance, where they would both excel.

Before studying dance, Glen Tetley (b. 1926) had initially studied anatomy and biology as part of a pre-medical curriculum. He began dancing relatively late, but became a leading performer with American Ballet Theatre, the Martha Graham Dance Company, and Jerome Robbins' Dance USA.

Tetley's debut as a choreographer was on May 5, 1962, when he presented an "An Evening of Theatre Dance" in the auditorium at the Fashion Institute of Technology in New York. Willa Kim's debut as a designer for dance occurred at the same time, with one of the pieces,

Tetley's *Birds of Sorrow*, danced to music by Peter Hartman. Tetley had dabbled with choreography before that time, doing small pieces for Alvin Ailey's company, just as Willa had been dabbling with costumes. But this was a major event that launched them both solidly into the dance world and into new careers—Willa Kim with dance-based costume design and Glen Tetley as a choreographer. The piece featured two men and a woman and was a modern dance version of a Japanese Noh play. In July 1962, it was performed again at Jacob's Pillow and was again acclaimed when danced by Linda Hodes, Robert Powell, and Glen Tetley himself.

One of the other pieces performed that same night, *Pierrot Lunaire,* has become a classic of the modern dance repertory. As a new designer, Willa Kim held her own with the productions by other designers who were more experienced: Beni Montressor, Rouben Ter-Arutunian, William Ritman, and Peter Harvey. These designers often did both sets and costumes, an example that Willa would follow when circumstances allowed. When Tetley and his dancers performed *Birds of Sorrow* for the Paris Ballet Festival later that year, her costume designs would be used again, and she would also design the setting for the performance.

Early in 1963, Arthur Kopit's *Asylum or What the Gentlemen Are Up to Not to Mention the Ladies* began rehearsals at Theater deLys. It was Kopit's new play, following the successful run of *Oh Dad, Poor Dad, Mama's Hung You in the Closet, and I'm Feeling So Sad*, so expectations were high. Gaynor Bradish directed the production with a cast of nineteen portraying famous people, among them Amelia Earhart and Joan of Arc, with Estelle Parsons in the later role. Previews were scheduled for February 22nd and the opening for March 10th, so the six-week rehearsal period was a busy one.

The costume shop was at Theater deLys and Willa had an office at the top of the stairs nearby. This was her first sustained backstage experience and it proved to be somewhat overwhelming to the theatre neophyte, whose main exposure to performers was through costumes displayed on dressmaker's mannequins and with fittings in established costume shops. Willa Kim confessed later that she wasn't even sure how to read and analyze a play. Indeed, this may well have been her first experience actually reading a new play, having listened to readings of *Red Eye of Love* both in Italy and during that play's rehearsal process. She had little understanding about backstage intrigues and knew even less about the relationships and hierarchy of the theatre. She didn't realize that when other members of the production team or the performers complained to her, they were just looking for a sympathetic ear. Clearly the play, set in an insane asylum, had difficulties that even the good will of producer Roger Stevens and set designer Hugh Hardy could not overcome. The play never opened.

But Willa continued designing costumes. Her activities in 1963 included the successful opening of *The Saving Grace*, a comedy by Edwin Harvey Blum starring John Cullum and Audree Rae on April 18, 1963 and an invitation from Robert Joffrey to design his new ballet, *Gamelan.*

The Robert Joffrey Ballet Company toured throughout the world and regularly performed throughout the United States. In winter 1962, the company went on a tour of the Far East under the auspices of the United States Cultural Presentations Program. A Soviet official saw a performance by the company in India and invited Robert Joffrey to bring his company on a tour of the Soviet Union, with performances beginning in the Kirov Theatre in Leningrad followed by appearances in Donetsk, Kharkov, Kiev, and ending in Moscow. For the Soviet tour, sponsored by the United States Department of State and the Rebekah Harkness Foundation, a number of new ballets were created by Robert Joffrey. One of the ballets was *Gamelan*, a series of short pieces with costumes by Willa Kim, sets by Ming Cho Lee, and lighting by Thomas Skelton. The music was composed by Lou Harrison for performance on traditional Javanese instruments. Joffrey's dance was vaguely Oriental and rather ritualistic (within a classical framework) but exceptionally beautiful and lyrical.

As a child, Robert Joffrey (1930-1988) had hoped to be a tap dancer, but instead began to study ballet in Seattle, Washington with Mary Ann Wells. One of his fellow students there was Gerald Arpino, who would later become his chief choreographer, co-company director, and after Joffrey's death, head of the Joffrey Ballet. Joffrey danced with Roland Petit's Ballets de Paris and in the early 1950s opened the American Dance Center. There he started to created ballets, including his first, *Persephone*. He formed his first company in 1954, the Robert Joffrey Ballet Concert. *Gamelan* was not performed in New York until September 8, 1965, at the Delacorte Theatre in Central Park, at a preview performance before an invited audience. The official opening was the following day.

The Robert Joffrey Ballet Company was formed in 1956. In 1966 the company became associated with the New York City Center and known as the City Center Joffrey Ballet. It performed regularly in New York City as well as in Los Angeles. In 1995 the company relocated to Chicago and was renamed the Joffrey Ballet.

During 1963 Miss Kim also designed costumes for *Funnyhouse of a Negro*, a work by the African-American playwright Adrienne Kennedy, which opened at the East End Theatre on January 14, 1964. The play was a brave and important one, confronting race and identity at the height of the Civil Rights Movement. The show's principals, director Michael Kahn and producers Richard Barr, Clinton Wilder, and Edward Albee, were justifiably proud of the result. For all its grittiness, in the end the play was a cause for celebration among the playgoers who flocked to

Funnyhouse of a Negro
Costume Design by Willa Kim. Ellen Holly as the Duchess of Hapsburg and Mary Alice as Queen Victoria, 1964. Courtesy of Willa Kim

see it. Billie Allen played the despairing central character, Sarah, who was so incapable of confronting the ghosts that inhabited her room and tormented her that she took her own life, the only relief she could imagine. This was not an easy play to design or watch, but it characterizes much of what Willa Kim would later choose to do—pieces that would invariably be interesting and compelling rather than easy. *Funnyhouse of a Negro* won the Obie Award for most distinguished play in the 1963-1964 season.

Soon after the opening of *Funnyhouse of a Negro*, Willa was presented with a new challenge. Arnold Weinstein, who a few short years before had convinced her to design costumes, was trying to convince her to do both sets and costumes for his new musical, *Dynamite Tonight!*, a collaboration with William Bolcom that was being produced by the Actors Studio Theatre. Why not?, she asked herself. She had started doing some backgrounds for ballets, and during her apprenticeship with Raoul Pène du Bois, she had watched him often do both sets and costumes. So why couldn't she?

When she was assisting Raoul Pène du Bois with costumes on many productions, he had often employed Mason Arvold as his assistant for scenery and Waldo Angelo as an additional assistant for costumes. She had spent long hours with them both as well as with Raoul, and had learned much. She also understood the art of scene design, the "painterly-ness" of scenery, and liked exerting her artistic vision as much possible. She would also be among friends, including Arnold Weinstein. Barbara Harris, Gene Wilder, and George Gaynes were in the cast, and the musical promised to be witty and imaginative. She agreed, and her sets and costumes were a success.

Birds of Sorrow
     (above) Costume Design by Willa Kim for Linda
     Hodes,1962. Choreography by Glen Tetley.
     Courtesy of Willa Kim.

Birds of Sorrow
     (top right) Costume Design by Willa Kim for
     Robert Powell, 1962. Choreography by Glen
     Tetley. Courtesy of Willa Kim.

Birds of Sorrow
     (bottom right) Costume Design by Willa Kim for
     Glen Tetley, 1962. Choreography by Glen
     Tetley. Courtesy of Willa Kim.

Weewis

Costume Rendering by Willa Kim for Jimmy Dunne and Gary Chryst, 1971. Choreography by Margo Sappington for the Joffrey Ballet. Courtesy of Willa Kim.

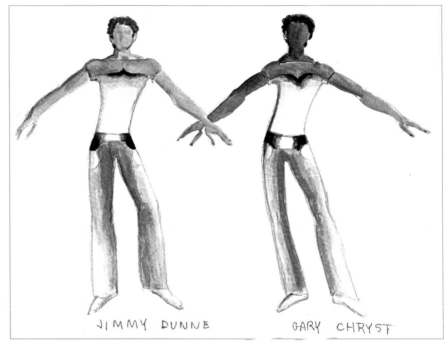

JIMMY DUNNE   GARY CHRYST

The Magic Flute

(below) Costume Design by Willa Kim for Rita Shane as "Queen of the Night," 1968. Courtesy of Willa Kim. Photograph by Alan Stoker.

Miss Kim made her formal debut as a designer of both sets and costumes for dance in the Robert Joffrey Ballet Company's premicre of *The Game of Noah*. As the title implies, the ballet concerned a children's game based on Noah's ark. It was choreographed to a series of pieces by Igor Stravinsky. The two dancers at the center of the piece, Alexandra Radius and Hans Ebbelaar, remain a couple beyond childhood, falling in love. The ballet got wonderful reviews as did the costumes and scenery designed by Willa Kim. When *The Game of Noah* had its American debut in August that same year, her sets and costumes were again complimented by critics in the major papers. This was also the first time she designed a costume for dancer Dennis Nahat, She would later design costumes for dances he choreographed and theatrical productions he directed.

Kim also designed costumes for other Joffrey Company-based choreographers, often dancers in his company, who were beginning to create pieces, including Margo Sappington, with whom she did *Weewis* in 1971, *Face Dancers* in 1976, and *Tactics* in 1976. For the company's chief choreographer, Gerald Arpino, she would do

The Magic Flute
Costume Design by Willa Kim for Evelyn Manda, Barbara Shuttleworth, and Jean Craft as "Attendants to the Queen of the Night," 1968. Courtesy of Willa Kim. Photograph by Alan Stoker.

The Magic Flute
Costume Rendering by Willa Kim for Attendants to the Queen of the Night, 1968. Courtesy of Willa Kim.

Nightwings in 1966, *Orpheus Times Light Squared* in 1976, and *Jamboree* in 1984.

In addition to the costumes, Willa Kim also designed scenery for *Orpheus Times Light Squared*. An unusual round shape dominates the space above the stage When asked where the idea for the shape came from, her eyes twinkle. Miss Kim wears a large flat silver ring on her right hand, often paired with an opaque silvery moon stone. The silver ring has a compelling and unusual shape that is not exactly a circle and not perfectly flat either. Like many of her costumes, it draws attention more to the movement of the hand wearing it than to itself. The ring is made out of an old British sterling silver coin that had been hammered (thus the shape) and attached to a band. When she began wearing the ring some of the original markings were still visible but over time they have been worn smooth. The scenery for *Orpheus Times Light Squared*, which opened at the City Center on October 21, 1976, owes its central motif to that ring.

With her reputation rapidly rising in the off-Broadway world, it came as no surprise that Willa Kim was asked to design costumes for the inaugural production of the American Place Theatre at St. Clements Church on West 46th Street. Founded by Wynn Handman, Sydney Lanier, and Michael Tolan in 1963, the American Place Theatre was formed to develop productions by writers not normally associated with the theatre. By 1964, the trio had a newly renovated space and were ready for a major production. A new trilogy by Robert Lowell, *The Old Glory: Endicott and the Red Cross, My Kinsman, Major Molineux* and *Benito Cereno*, was chosen and Jonathan Miller was hired to direct. During rehearsals it became apparent that three plays were too many, and so *Endicott and the Red Cross* was cut.

The notices were excellent, especially for *Benito Cereno*. Interviewed later that year in the *New York Times* (December 6, 1964), Jonathan Miller credited Willa Kim with much of the production's success: "They [the actors] were helped, of course, by the flaring invention of Willa Kim's extraordinary costumes. These were being made and designed in the theatre itself so that the actors could see their future selves growing daily before their eyes." Others agreed, and early in 1965, Willa Kim received the first of her many awards for costume design, the 1964-1965 Obie Award for outstanding costume design for *The Old Glory*.

In October 1965, NET (National Educational Television) broadcast *Benito Cereno* over Channel 13 in New York City, bringing the production into thousands of homes. Willa Kim had already designed other productions for television, including *St. Patrick's Day* by Robert Sheridan for the Esso Repertory Theatre.

Miss Kim's renown continued to grow. She designed additional off-Broadway plays including *Helen* by Wallace Gray, starring Katharine Balfour. In summer 1965 she designed her first opera, the United States premiere of Hans Werner Henze's *The Stag King* for the Santa Fe Opera. The production was an enormous success, as directed by Bliss Hebert, with rave notices in the *New York Times* soon after the production opened and again during the run, urging New Yorkers to make the trip to Santa Fe. The first notice (August 8, 1965) suggested that "Her medieval court dress had the opulence of an expensive Broadway musical, and she had a field day creating hats and headdresses of whimsical shapes and sizes." This was quite a compliment for someone who had not yet designed a Broadway show. The second review (August 22, 1965) went even further, saying "The fantastic creatures in "The Stag King," magnificently costumed by Willa Kim, seemed to float on stage from the surrounding night."

Willa Kim's first Broadway show was *Malcolm* by Edward Albee, whom she had met when designing *Funnyhouse of a Negro*. The production featured Matthew Cowles in the title role, Estelle Parsons as Laureen, and Jennifer West as a very successful rock and roll singer who wore especially inventive costumes. The venture to Broadway was a success for all involved, and not only was Willa engaged for additional productions at a rapid pace, she was sought out for feature articles in newspapers and magazines.

Eugenia Sheppard, Women's Features editor for the *New York Herald Tribune*, interviewed Willa for an article in the paper's home section. They discussed the skimpy, attractive, short-short skirts, beads, and feathers Jennifer West wore in the show, portraying a blonde bombshell. During the interview published on January 4, 1966, Willa suggested that one of the costumes for the leading lady in *Malcolm* looked like it had "bubbles under the arms" because of the presence of numerous ruffles filling in her cleavage. That phrase ended up as the title of the article and in the illustrations that accompanied it. The illustrations were not Willa's original designs, but rather ones done by illustrator and sometime costume designer Joe Eula. When columnist Art Buchwald saw the illustrations in the *Herald Tribune* he responded with a column also called, "Bubbles under the arms" which was published on January 20, 1966.

This visibility led to additional exposure. The September 7, 1968 issue of *The New Yorker* magazine ran a full page advertisement for Ballantyne cashmere sweaters on page 21 with the caption, "Who is this famous couple?" The now-famous couple was costume designer Willa Kim, and her husband, artist and illustrator William Pène du Bois.

In 1966, the New York City Center of Music and Drama added the Joffrey Ballet to its roster of resident professional companies. The new season for the Joffrey (renamed the City Center Joffrey Ballet) began on September 6, 1966, at the 55th Street Theatre. On the program that opening night was the premiere of *Nightwings*, choreographed by Gerald Arpino, and a revised version of Robert Joffrey's *Gamelan*.

Both ballets featured costumes by Willa Kim, who was continuing to develop what would become her signature design elements: "a whiff of period" and "a suggestion of place." Always her designs served the movement of the dance. Kim developed the habit of seeing dances before designing them, so as to capture their essence, as she did in the bird-like white headdress designed for Lisa Bradley for *Nightwings*.

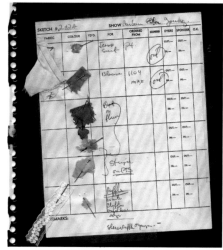

Operation Sidewinder
   Fabric plot by Willa Kim for "Honey" costume, 1970. Courtesy of Willa Kim.

Operation Sidewinder
   Costume Rendering by Willa Kim for Barbara eda-Young as "Honey," 1970. Courtesy of Willa Kim.

Operation Sidewinder
   Costume Rendering by Willa Kim for Robert Phalen as "Dukie," 1970. Courtesy of Willa Kim.

Operation Sidewinder
   Costume Rendering by Willa Kim for Don Plumley as "Mickey Free," 1970. Courtesy of Willa Kim.

scout masters hat

army jacket
decorated with
shells tufts of hair
fringe. stolen
jewelry-watches.
fobs. teeth.
fingers-

dress
shirt

pouch

loin
cloth

OPERATION SIDEWINDER
APACHE #2

Operation Sidewinder
Costume Rendering by Willa Kim for "Apache #2," 1970. Courtesy of
Willa Kim.

Help! Help! The Globolinks
Scenic Design by Willa Kim, 1969. Santa Fe Opera Company. Courtesy of Willa Kim.

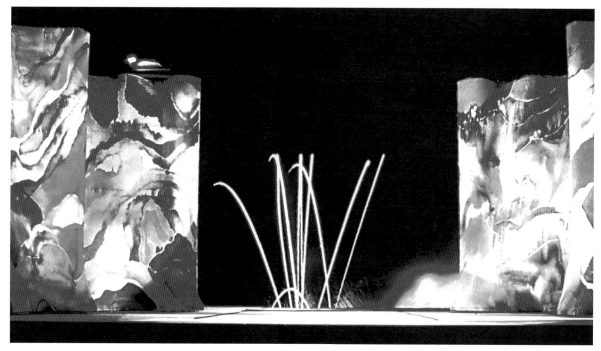

Two months later, Miss Kim's designs appeared in another Broadway production, David Halliwell's *Hail, Scrawdyke!*, directed by Alan Arkin. The play, which opened at the Booth Theatre on November 28, 1966, featured Victor Henry as the antihero Malcolm Scrawdyke, and made a star of Austin Pendleton, who played the character Irwin Ingham.

The following year she designed a new ballet, the *Seven Deadly Sins*, for Glen Tetley and his company. The work was premiered that summer at the Vancouver (Canada) Festival accompanied by a live performance by the Vancouver Symphony Orchestra. Willa Kim also returned to the American Place Theatre at St. Clement's Church to design *The Ceremony of Innocence* by Ronald Ribman. Directed by Arthur A. Seidelman, the play opened on December 14, 1967.

The year 1968 saw Willa Kim's triumphant return to the Santa Fe Opera Company for a new production of *The Magic Flute*. Her designs for *The Stag King*, her first opera, had been very well received, and she relished the chance to return to the operatic form, which allowed her to exercise her creative imagination in new ways.

The staging of *The Magic Flute* that year in Santa Fe was a special one for everyone involved, because the theatre used by the company had burned to the ground the previous summer. The opening performance of Mozart's opera would be among those to inaugurate the new and enlarged theatre. While the production values in Santa Fe had always been high, the improved costume workroom and scene shop areas built for the new theatre made it possible to mount productions on an even larger scale. Indeed, everything about this production would be new, as the sets and costumes for earlier productions of the opera had been destroyed in the fire.

Bliss Hebert, who had first worked with Willa Kim on *The Stag King* at Santa Fe in 1965, directed *The Magic Flute*. In his staging, the Queen of the Night wears a crown that evokes the moon. From the viewpoint of the audience seated in the half-open-air theatre, it seemed as if the moon was rising on the stage as the Queen of the Night entered, apparently

Le Rossignol: Stravinsky Remembered
  Costume and Set Design by Willa Kim. Santa Fe Opera (1969) for National Educational Television, 1971. Courtesy of Willa Kim.

floating over the stage and accompanied by her three attendants. Miss Kim dressed the bird-seller Papageno and his counterpart Papagena in a flurry of feathers and fruit. Their costumes became even more convincing during the course of the opera, when in Hebert's staging of Mozart, the pair sing and mimic birdsong.

With the huge success of *The Magic Flute*, Willa Kim and Bliss Hebert were signed on to stage two productions for the 1969 season, the United States premiere of Gian Carlo Menotti's *Help! Help! The Globolinks*, and Igor Stravinsky's *Le Rossignol*. Miss Kim designed both sets and costumes for each of these one-act shows, which were performed together at Santa Fe.

The pairing of the two productions was a clever choice by the legendary John Crosby, who founded, managed, and often conducted the orchestra during performances by the Santa Fe Opera Company. Menotti's more traditional music in his parable about the dangers of industrialization and mechanization contrasted with the avant-garde Stravinsky, who transformed Hans Christian Andersen's legend of ancient China, "The Emperor and the Nightingale." Willa Kim's Asian heritage, which has often been cited as underpinning her composed yet witty style, was clearly valued by Bliss Hebert for this production. Her design of stylized clouds and trees over a Chinese court was itself a parable about the transformative power of the Nightingale when faced by Death.

When *Le Rossignol* was filmed for television in 1971 at the studios of WNET in New York City, Miss Kim once again designed both sets and costumes, transforming the elements from the expansive Santa Fe stage to the far smaller studio at Channel 13. To commemorate the death of Igor Stravinsky, who had died on April 6, 1971, the production was broadcast on November 22, 1971, on National Educational Television. One of the clouds that Willa Kim designed for that production still hangs in her home, continuing to evoke the magical world of ancient China that she had created.

A year earlier, Willa Kim had designed a work for Sam Shepard. His theatre career had begun with Theatre Genesis' production of two one-act plays, *Cowboys* and *The Rock Garden*, at

St. Mark's Church-in-the-Bowery in 1964. His first full-length play, *La Turista*, was performed at the American Place Theatre in 1967. In 1970, he was still considered a promising young playwright when *Operation Sidewinder* opened on March 12th, at Lincoln Center's Vivian Beaumont Theatre. It's not clear that the critics (or audiences for that matter) completely understood the play, an allegory about American consumerism in the guise of snakes and lizards. The sidewinder in the title refers to a top secret U.S. Air Force project in which a computer is disguised as a sidewinder, an indigenous snake. Complications ensue when the native peoples of the desert begin to worship the reptile. A marvelous mechanical snake, designed by Jean Delasser, complimented Willa Kim's path-breaking costume designs.

When she designed the production, Miss Kim created a very specific pattern on the costume for the character "Honey" to be played by Barbara eda-Young. She naturally wanted the dress to look exactly like the rendering, but the costume makers at Eaves Costume Company, were uncertain about the best way to create the designs on the garment. None of the fabric swatches available in the five boroughs of New York were similar to what she had painted. Moreover, the costume makers' experiments with painting the design onto cloth made the initially soft fabrics stiff and ungainly. Willa knew that painting on soft fabrics had to be possible. Where, she asked, were silk-screening techniques being used to print patterns onto dresses?

Andrew Geoly, the head of the Eaves Costume Company, happened to mention Willa Kim's question to his golfing buddies, several of whom had connections in the rag trade. One of the men was using a silk screen technique to produce bolts of cloth with designs similar to those made popular by the bold patterns and colors of Emilio Pucci (1914-1992). It seemed possible that a similar process using the same inks might work on a smaller scale for a costume.

When Geoly relayed this information to the costume makers, it was not a shopper or an assistant who took the subway to Brooklyn to explore the possibilities, but Willa herself. After touring the factory she talked the manager into giving her some containers of dye in the colors she wanted and returned with them to Eaves.

With Barbara eda-Young modeling the dress which had been made from the right weight fabric from a solid color that would form the background, Willa drew her designs over the entire garment, designating which colors were to be used in each area. When the garment was completely silk-screened it looked exactly like the original sketch.

Willa Kim's insistence on reproducing her costume designs exactly as they were shown on her sketches led her to create an entirely new way of painting and dyeing costumes, which has become the industry standard. It was the first time that a costume design had been reproduced on a garment while retaining the suppleness of the fabric. This also marked the beginning of one of Willa Kim's signature design elements: custom-painted costumes. She had begun to more fully integrate her skills as a painter and an illustrator into her theatrical designs. The effects that she had created would soon start a revolution when applied to dance costumes.

In November 1970 alone, Willa Kim had two ballets and a play begin their performances. The *Sunday Dinner*, Joyce Carol Oates' first play, opened on November 2, 1970, at St. Clement's Church in New York, produced by the American Place Theatre. It was directed by Curt Dempster and featured Jacqueline Brookes and Patrick McVey in a play about a particularly miserable family.

Brahms Quintet, with costumes by Willa Kim and choreography by Dennis Nahat, opened on November 10, 1970, at the King's Theatre in Stockholm, when The Royal Swedish Ballet added the piece to its repertoire. The ballet had been created for the American Ballet Theatre and was first performed on December 10, 1969. *Brahms Quintet* has remained a popular ballet, with the original choreography and costumes by Nahat and Kim retained by such companies as the Cleveland Ballet Company and Ballet San Jose.

On November 29, 1970, *Ontogeny*, also with choreography by Dennis Nahat and costumes by Willa Kim, received its world premiere. The ballet featured Czech-born composer Karel Husa's Third String Quartet, which had won the Pulitzer Prize for Music the previous year. The American Ballet Theatre began performing the piece on January 6, 1971, when the work had its American premiere at the New York City Center with a performance by the American Ballet Theatre.

Willa Kim's visibility in the world of theatre and ballet continued to rise, as did her social profile. The world of dance and theatre is not one of regular hours, so hospitality for Willa could be a meal cooked for friends in the middle of the afternoon or in the middle of the night. The October 1971 issue of *McCall's* magazine featured three two-page spreads about three busy career women—Willa Kim, Pia Lindstrom, and Jane Trahey—who none-the-less managed to throw parties. The article, "Entertaining: The Second 30 Years, It Gets Easier," includes a large photograph of carefully cooked and arranged Korean food, with Willa posed on a high-backed wicker chair, rather Asian in design. In front of her is a table is filled with dishes, many of them "Willowware" from her own cupboards. They are filled with Korean food such as *kim chee* (Korean pickle) and *bul-kogi* (Korean barbecued beef). Miss Kim wears a ruffled shirt that was the prototype for a costume for one of the male dancers in the Swedish Ballet's production of *Brahms Quintet*. The entire scene looks charming and artistic, and she looks like the gracious hostess her friends continue to report her to be.

The story is told that when Willa arrived at the McCall's studios for the initial photo shoot, she scrutinized the way that the photographer had arranged the food. Quickly she reached for a butcher knife and cut a wedge out of a stem of Romaine lettuce situated on a platter. (Lettuce is often used for wrapping Korean food, especially *bul-kogi*, to make it easier to eat with the fingers.) When she returned a few days later for the final shoot, the assistants helping to set up the display asked her to make that special "Korean cooking" cut on the lettuce leaves again. She made the v-shaped cut even though the lettuce was perfectly fine and the v-shaped slice wasn't a feature of Korean cuisine at all. She had simply seen a blemish on the lettuce, and had cut it out.

The year 1971 saw Willa Kim collaborate with a new choreographer, on a ballet to be called *Weewis*. Margo Sappington had been a dancer with the Joffrey Ballet and other companies, and would become a successful choreographer. Her achievements have been somewhat overshadowed by her association with the notorious production of *Oh! Calcutta!* in which she danced as well as choreographed. Willa Kim had dressed Margo when she danced with Robert Joffrey, and so it was logical that when Margo began choreographing she would turn to Willa as a costume designer. Their first collaboration opened on October 27, 1971, at the New York City Center. The critics were unanimous in their praise for Willa, citing her "excellent colored costumes." (NYT November 21, 1971)

The costumes for the ballet were to be made at the Studio, located on West 14th Street in New York, by Betty Williams, one of the founders of the famed costume cooperative. Willa had shown the designs to Betty, who would decide the best method and the best materials to use. She showed Willa a new fabric that she had found, and asked if she would be willing to look at her designs made up in the rather elastic new fabric, which previously had only been used in foundation garments. The material was Lycra Spandex, which has come to be known by a variety of terms, including milliskin, lycra, and spandex. It began to be used commercially in 1962, initially for girdles. The underwear maker, Warner's, was among the first to aggressively advertise that they made their foundation garments from this new fiber, which not only stretched but recovered its original shape. The fiber, an elastomeric synthetic, was invented by Joseph C. Shivers for E.I. du Pont de Nemours and Company in 1959.

Betty Williams (1931-1997) was a New York-based costumer for nearly forty years. She made the costumes for the original productions of *The Fantastics*, *Oh! Calcutta* (meeting Margo Sappington in the process), and hundreds more. Miss Williams had extended relationships with the New York City Opera, the Alvin Ailey Dance Company, the Jose Limon Company, and the Joffrey Ballet. She created original dressmaker patterns and started an extensive collection of historical commercial patterns, and, in the 1970s, pioneered the use of stretch materials for dance with the costumes in her workrooms for *Weewis*, designed by Willa Kim. Soon afterwards, Betty produced a commercial pattern for leotards that by the mid-1970s was being used throughout the United States in commercial and amateur costume shops.

The Drama Desk Award statue is not especially large, nor one that has much recognition beyond the entertainment industry, but the one that Willa Kim won for *The Screens* in 1972 was big enough to confirm—to her and everyone else in the business that she was a success. During her first ten years in the business she had designed costumes for some fifty plays and ballets and was starting to be recognized, not just by the inner circle of dance and theatre aficionados, but by critics and prize juries.

The Screens received its American premiere at the Brooklyn Academy of Music on

'LEILA'
"THE SCREENS"
JEAN GENET

The Screens
Costume Rendering by Willa Kim for Janet League as
"Leila," 1971. Courtesy of Willa Kim.

November 30, 1971. It was directed by Minos Volanakis and presented by the Chelsea Theatre Center of Brooklyn, an organization known for its adventurous productions. The play, which featured a large cast and lasted nearly five hours, was not the kind of work audiences see for an evening of pleasure and escape. It was, however, one of the biggest theatrical events of the year, and audiences flocked to see Julie Bovasso, Robert Jackson, and Janet League. In his review the following day in the *New York Times* (December 13, 1971), Clive Barnes recommended the production as an "almost monumental achievement" and praised the design, saying that "Willa Kim's costumes admirably convey the play's tatterdemalion nature and air of decay."

Miss Kim not only won the Drama Desk Award for outstanding costume design, she also received the *Variety* New York Drama Critics Poll Award and the Maharam Award. Two of Willa Kim's costume designs, for the Judge (John Capodice) and the Mother (Julie Bovasso) were reproduced in a story about the production in the June 17, 1972 edition of the *Saturday Review*.

In subsequent years, Willa Kim would refer to the time between 1963 and 1976 as her "Joffrey Years" for good reason. She designed several ballets, including *Gamelan* (1963), *Game of Noah* (1965), *Weewis* (1971), *Jive* (1973), *Nightwings* (1966), *Remembrances* (1973), *Tactics* (1976), *Orpheus Times Light Squared* (1976), and *Face Dancers* (1976). Perhaps no ballet was more important to her developing career than *Jive* in 1973, because it was the first ballet she designed for Eliot Feld, who was at the time starting to develop as a choreographer and with whom she would ultimately collaborate on more than sixty pieces. One of the Joffrey administrators, Bill Crawford, had recommended Willa Kim to Eliot Feld, who to this day counts her among his chief influences and collaborators. "There have been times," he says, "when not only did she understand a dance, she explained it to me." (NYT November 28, 1986)

Eliot Feld was born in Brooklyn, and studied at the School of American Ballet and with the New Dance Group. He appeared, at age twelve, as the Child Prince in George Balanchine's original staging of *The Nutcracker* for the New York City Ballet. As a dancer he performed with the American Ballet Theatre, Pearl Lang, Sophie Maslow, Donald McKayle and others, and on Broadway he performed in *West Side Story* among other musicals. In 1968 Feld formed his own company, the American Ballet Company and in 1973 he reorganized that company into the Eliot Feld Ballet. The first collaborations between Kim and Feld were for the Joffrey Ballet.

Even though the Robert Joffrey Ballet Company was having financial problems in 1973 that threatened the company's future, its artistic achievements that spring season were considerable. Twyla Tharp choreographed a new piece, *Deuce Coupe*; Eliot Feld contributed *Jive*; and the company revived a 1917 cubist masterpiece, *Parade*, on March 22, 1973, at the New York City Center.

The original choreography for *Parade* was by Léonide Massine (1896-1979), who had based the ballet on a libretto by Jean Cocteau. Erik Satie had composed the music, and Pablo Picasso had designed the sets and costumes. Willa Kim's long-standing relationship and solid reputation with the company made her the perfect choice to supervise the construction of Picasso's original designs for the Chinese Conjurer, a troupe of acrobats, and the American Girl. Kermit Love recreated the French and American Managers and a stage horse, each of which was more an architectural construction than a costume. Bill Crawford recreated the choreography with Massine himself supervising the reconstruction of the dance, with assistance from Douglas Cooper, Picasso's biographer. The illustrations that Cooper was able to provide were especially helpful to Edward Burbridge, who was responsible for the reconstruction of the set. All the design team had to work with were old black and white photographs and a few faded color slides of the original curtain.

Although Miss Kim was clearly pleased with the costumes for *Parade* at the time, in later years she allowed herself to brag a bit, noting to friends that she had indeed "got them right." She had been able to create a pair of thick-soled slippers and a hat for the Chinese Conjurer that Picasso had originally designed, but that had not been produced for the original Paris production. According to Léonide Massine, the costume makers could not devise what Picasso had envisioned. And because the few available photographs of the Paris production did not show all aspects of the original costumes, Kim had to provide new designs for the missing portions, which included most of the back views. In her recreation of Picasso's designs Willa Kim had returned in a sense to the way she had worked in the early 1950s, when she had had helped other designers realize their own designs.

Widely regarded as exacting by her fellow professionals, Willa Kim always pursues perfection in the realization of her designs. She demands that the costumes look like the sketches, that the colors match her paintings, and that the fabrics be the correct fiber and of the proper weight.

The Screens
Costume Rendering by Willa Kim for Rob Jackson as "Said," 1971. Courtesy of Willa Kim.

During her apprenticeship with Karinska and Raoul Pène du Bois she had learned well the lesson that the artistry in a costume rendering was faithfully translated onto the stage by personal attention to every detail.

Because of her preference for fabrics that drape and move beautifully, it surprised some members of the dance community that Willa Kim was so instrumental in promoting the use of synthetic, elastomeric materials for dance costumes. Kim acknowledges that her use of fabric is somewhat intuitive. When she touches a piece of cloth—or sometimes when she sees it—she knows if it will be appropriate or not.

For the fall season in New York in 1973, Robert Joffrey choreographed *Remembrances* for his company. Joffrey used the suite of music that Richard Wagner had composed for Mathilde Wesendonck, including the five lieder. It featured two of his dancers, Jonathan Watts and Francesca Corkle, as a couple performing romantic variations of embracing and separating. Joffrey wanted Willa to design the costumes for the ballet, with the same fabric she had used for *Weewis* in 1971. She did not immediately agree because she wanted to see the dance before deciding what the costumes might look like or considering what fabrics to use in their construction. After seeing their movements, she agreed to design the ballet using the synthetic stretchy material.

The costumes for *Remembrances* were made by Sally Ann Parsons who had worked at Ray Diffen's Studio making dance costumes before becoming a partner in Parsons-Meares, Ltd. She had made costumes for Willa for other productions, but when she made the costumes for *Remembrances* she used the elastomeric fiber Lycra Spandex for the first time. Within a few short years spandex would become a popular fabric for dance, exercise, and sport use, and within ten years it would dominate the materials used for those activities.

Before the mid-1970s, bias-cut fabrics—mainly wool jersey—and some early forms of nylon such as Helanca nylon—were the common materials used for dance. Helanca was developed in Switzerland by American Rudolph Kaegi in the early 1930s; he created this first real stretch fabric by combining wool with Celanese, a cellulose acetate fiber. The stretch quality remained intact until a garment was washed. Heberlein & Co., refined Helanca in the early 1950s by combining nylon rather than acetate with wool.

In 1952, Maria Bogner (1914-2002) revolutionized ski-wear when she began marketing ski-pants made from Helanca. They were a huge success, especially when made in bright colors. Once Burlington Industries was licensed to manufacture Helanca in the U.S. in 1955, the fabric became generally available and was quickly adopted for dancewear, although the wool content was much better suited to the ski slopes than the dance studio. When dances required considerable extension of arms or legs, those limbs were often left uncovered.

With the availability of fabrics made from fibers that were less warm to wear and that could stretch and then return to their original shape, specifically Lycra Spandex, dance costume was again transformed. Designer Willa Kim, and costume makers Ray Diffen, Sally Ann Parsons, and Betty Williams were the true pioneers.

Long before Danskin and Capezio were marketing garments made from stretchy synthetic fabrics, Betty Williams and Sally Ann Parsons were producing original dance costumes to the specifications of Willa Kim's designs. It had not taken long for Willa Kim to combine the painting technique she had developed for *Operation Sidewinder* with the stretch materials she used for *Weewis*. By painting on stretch fabrics, the costumes used for dancers throughout the world were transformed. The designs for dance costumes were enhanced by her painting techniques and they fit better, much to the pleasure of audiences and performers alike. The painted costumes also retained their bright colors through necessary and repeated cleanings much better than dyed ones, especially after Willa Kim developed a method for using steam to set the colors. Fading had been a difficulty Willa encountered when she painted images—by hand—from the comics pages onto the costumes for *The Old Glory* in 1964.

Among the artisans who worked extensively with Miss Kim as painters were Parmalee Wells, Richard Hornung, and Brian Kolman. Wells in particular was part of the early development of the process while Hornung and Kolman painted numerous garments to Kim's specification and under her close scrutiny.

Willa Kim soon made a transition from dance premieres to theatrical ones—from spandex to Stoppard. The American premiere of *Jumpers* by Tom Stoppard occurred on February 18, 1974 at the Kennedy Center for the Performing Arts, in Washington, D.C. where it played prior to the opening on Broadway. Tom Stoppard's first major success was with *Rosencrantz and Guildenstern are Dead* in 1966. Prior to that he had worked as a journalist and had written some radio and television plays.

Peter Wood directed *Jumpers*, but Willa Kim's involvement with the production was due to producer Roger Stevens, who she first worked with in 1963 on Arthur Kopit's aborted play, *Asylum or What the Gentlemen Are Up to Not to Mention the Ladies*. While Stevens was pleased to be associated with her once again, Dennis Nahat was delighted. Their first collaboration on choreography and costumes had been for *Brahms Quintet* in 1969. Matching the witty Stoppard with the equally clever Kim was a useful combination.

More ballets followed, including two for New York's Harkness Ballet. Willa designed costumes for Norman Walker's *Ceremonials*, which opened on April 9, 1974, and both sets and costumes for *Rodin, Mis En Vie*, which opened on April 17, 1974. *Rodin, Mis En Vie*, with choreography by Margo Sappington, brought Rodin's sculptures to life during the hour-long ballet, set to music by composer Michael Kamen. In his review for the *New York Times* (April 19, 1974), Clive Barnes remarked: "Willa Kim's costumes, flesh-colored leotards beautifully touched in with colored hints of musculature, suggest nudity most admirably." He continued: "I also liked Miss Kim's scaffolding and aluminum-foil apotheosis that seemed to suggest both a sculptor's atelier and a setting for his cataclysmic vision."

Some years later, Willa Kim would alternate between delight and chagrin when repeating a story about being in a fitting room and overhearing a conversation in an adjacent room where the technique created to "suggest nudity so admirably" as Clive Barnes said, was being urged on another designer. She had insisted that the costume shop create a very specific design for her, inserting small circles of a shiny texture into the matte fabric of an existing unitard, and even helped them develop the methods to do it. When listening to her ideas being claimed as the property of someone else, she told herself to be philosophical and accept that "imitation is the sincerest form of flattery." In reality it bothered Miss Kim that the technique she invented was not only being appropriated by the costume makers in that shop, but that it was also being urged on her competition.

The year 1974 also saw Willa Kim's debut as a designer of costumes for figure skaters. Janet Lynn had won five consecutive U.S. National figure-skating titles from 1969 to 1973, and a bronze medal at the 1972 Olympics in Sapporo, Japan. After finishing second during the 1973 world championships, Janet Lynn turned professional and agreed to star in the *Ice Follies*, produced by Shipstads and Johnson, during their 1974-1975 tour. Lynn's agent, who had seen Willa Kim's dance designs, tracked her down and convinced her to design the four costumes that Janet Lynn would wear for the *Ice Follies*. Designing for an ice skater proved to be much like designing for a dancer, and the relationship was a success. Willa Kim would go on to design for other figure skaters including John Curry and Yuka Sato.

In the spring of 1975, Willa Kim's costumes were back on Broadway, this time for the musical *Goodtime Charley* by Sidney Michaels. The show opened on March 3, 1975, at the Palace Theatre, with music by Larry Grossman and Hal Hackaday. Though the play received mixed reviews from critics and had a relatively short run, it did manage to garner Tony Award nominations for its stars Joel Grey and Ann Reinking, and Richard B. Shull (Featured Actor) and Susan Browning (Best Featured Actress). The production also earned Tony Award nominations for its three principal designers, Rouben Ter-Arutunian (scene design), Abe Feder (lighting design), and Willa Kim (costume design).

While Willa Kim was working on the costumes for *Goodtime Charley*, a young choreographer was working on a new ballet in California. Michael Smuin, a Montanan who had been a principal dancer and choreographer with the American Ballet Theatre, had moved to California in 1973 to become director of the San Francisco Ballet. He had become fascinated with Japanese culture during a tour of that country with American Ballet Theatre. As early as 1973 he had wanted to create a ballet that didn't have a happy ending, and found the *shinjū* tradition appropriate. He commissioned music from Paul Seiko Chihara and adapted a nineteenth-century Japanese tale using elements from both Kabuki and Noh drama. Smuin wanted to create a ballet featuring highly stylized movement built around a story about an ill-fated love affair that ends in a double suicide.

Michael Smuin wanted Willa Kim to design sets and costumes for the ballet *Shinjū* and called her to make an offer. She declined, explaining that she was busy designing *Goodtime Charlie* for Broadway and *Daphnis and Chloe* for choreographer Glen Tetley, which was scheduled to open in June 1975 at the Wuerttemberg State Theatre in Stuttgart, Germany. Smuin called again and urged her to reconsider mentioning several designs he had seen and liked, including *Le Rossignol* and *Gamelan*, and telling her how much he admired them. She refused again, but a few days later agreed to see Smuin's dancers during a rehearsal of the piece. In between fittings for Joel Grey and Ann Reinking, Willa flew to San Francisco. After seeing the dancers rehearse she agreed to design costumes and scenery for *Shinjū*. Miss Kim flew back to New York, designed the production, and had the costumes made in New York.

Mr. Smuin believed in Willa Kim's design instincts. He later told her that he "trusted that she would design the dance he choreographed." The costumes and scenery were indeed brilliant. The San Francisco Ballet Company program for the 1975/1976 season contains a long article about the evolution of the ballet by Renee Renouf. "Michael had an unerring choice for his costume and set designer—Willa Kim, American born of Korean descent. His brows raised slightly when he spoke of her and his voice was faintly tinged with awe. 'She is pretty choosy about accepting offers and she only accepts about four a year.'" The author also observed that "Kim's part of the production deepened it, taking a tradition and making just enough of a fantasy from it to lift it from the formalized Japanese theatre without destroying the traditional structure indicated by some costume shapes."

Shinjū opened on March 20, 1975, at San Francisco's War Memorial Opera House. Willa Kim was there and stood on the stage at the end of the ballet, arm and arm with Michael Smuin, the principal dancers—Denis de Coteau, Tina Santos, and Gary Wahl—and composer Paul Chihara. Smuin and Kim celebrated their success and immediately began making plans for their next project.

Impromptu
Costume Design by Willa Kim for Birgit Keil, 1976. Choreography by Eliot Feld for The Feld Ballet. Courtesy of Willa Kim.

Dancin'
Costume Rendering by Willa Kim for Karen Burke, 1978. Courtesy of Willa
Kim. Photo by Jan Juracek.

Dancin'
Costume Designs by Willa Kim for (left to right) Wayne Cilento, Christopher Chadman, and John Mineo, 1978. Courtesy of Willa Kim. Photo © Martha Swope.

Next, however, came the Stuttgart Ballet's world premiere of *Daphnis and Chloe* in Germany on May 17, 1975, followed by the American premiere on June 12, 1975 at the Metropolitan Opera House. (Miss Kim also designed the poster for the Stuttgart Ballet's performances in May 1975.) In addition to Tetley's *Daphnis and Chloe*, Eliot Feld's *Intermezzo* (1969) and Jirí Kylián's *Rükkehr ins Fremde Land* completed the three-ballet program. It was in Stuttgart that Miss Kim first met Czech dancer and choreographer Jirí Kylián, with whom she would later collaborate.

Willa Kim also designed costumes for Margo Sappington's *Face Dancers* which the Joffrey Ballet opened on February 1, 1976, at the New York City Center and created costumes for the American Place Theatre's revival of *The Old Glory*, which opened on April 9, 1976. The revival included all three one-act plays, including *Endicott and the Red Cross*, which had been cut from the premiere performances due to the length of the event. *The Old Glory* had been the inaugural production when the American Place Theatre began performing at St. Clement's Church in 1964. The revival marked the opening of the American Place Theatre's new theatre space on the lower levels of a high-rise office building at 111 West 46th Street in New York.

Goodtime Charley
Costume Rendering by Willa Kim for Joel Grey as "Charley," Act I, scene 2, 1975. Courtesy of Willa Kim.

LEG OF MUTTON
SLEEVE

PEAS

KEYS, LADEL
POTATOS.
LARGE

CHECKER BOARD
PAINTED - APPLIQUED

SAINY (LIKE ENAMEL)

MOLDING.

"GOODTIME CHARLEY"

SK 81   COOK CHUCK RULE

1975

Goodtime Charley
Costume Rendering by Willa Kim for Chuck Rule as "Cook," 1975.
Courtesy of Willa Kim.

A Footstep of Air

(top left) Costume Design by Willa Kim for Linda Miller, 1977. Choreography by Eliot Feld for The Feld Ballet Courtesy of Willa Kim. Photo © Lois Greenfield.

A Footstep of Air

(bottom left) Costume Design by Willa Kim for Edmund LaFosse, 1977. Choreography by Eliot Feld for The Feld Ballet. Courtesy of Willa Kim. Photo © Lois Greenfield.

A Footstep of Air

(below) Costume Design by Willa Kim for Eliot Feld, 1977. Choreography by Eliot Feld for The Feld Ballet. Courtesy of Willa Kim. Photo © Lois Greenfield.

Willa Kim had by this time designed costumes for major dance companies on both coasts and for the Santa Fe Opera. Her reputation had spread throughout the country, as dance companies toured, directors worked in a variety of locations, and televised versions reached a large audience, particularly via the Public Broadcasting System's *Dance in America* series. When the Pennsylvania Ballet Company commissioned Margo Sappington to create a ballet, she choreographed *Under the Sun*, a work which recalled the movement of Alexander Calder's mobiles. Sappington asked Willa Kim to design the costumes, which according to the *New York Times* dance critic Anna Kisselgoff were "beautiful tights touched by typical Calder colors." (NYT October 21, 1976)

Under the Sun opened in Philadelphia at the Shubert Theatre on October 7, 1976 and was subsequently performed by the Pennsylvania Ballet at the Brooklyn Academy of Music, beginning on October 20, 1976. When the Philadelphia Museum of Art opened its Calder Celebration on December 11, 1982, Willa Kim's original costume designs were part of the museum's exhibit.

If the period from the mid-1960s to the mid-1970s were her "Joffrey years," then the "Feld years" began on October 20, 1976, when *Impromptu* marked the formation of The Feld Ballet with a performance at the Newman Theatre at the New York Shakespeare Festival. Although Willa Kim had designed for Eliot Feld when his pieces were performed by the Joffrey companies and by the American Ballet Theatre, once Feld established his own company, Miss Kim became his major contributor of costume designs, amassing over sixty

Under the Sun
 Costume Rendering by Willa Kim for Joanne Danto, 1976. Choreography by Margo Sappington for Pennsylvania Ballet's *Calder Celebration*. Courtesy of Willa Kim.

Under the Sun
 Costume Rendering by Willa Kim for Janek Schergen, 1976. Choreography by Margo Sappington for Pennsylvania Ballet's *Calder Celebration*. Courtesy of Willa Kim.

Shinjū

(left) Costume Design by Willa Kim for Anton Ness, 1975. Choreography by Michael Smuin for San Francisco Ballet. Courtesy of Willa Kim. Photo © Dan Esgro.

Shinjū

(above) Costume Design by Willa Kim for Michael Dwyer and Paula Tracy, 1975. Choreography by Michael Smuin for San Francisco Ballet. Courtesy of Willa Kim. Photo © Arne Folkedal.

Under the Sun

(left) Costume Rendering by Willa Kim for Missy Yancey, 1976. Choreography by Margo Sappington for Pennsylvania Ballet's Calder Celebration. Courtesy of Willa Kim.

Papillon
Costume Design by Willa Kim for Two Butterflies, 1979. Choreography
by Eliot Feld for The Feld Ballet. Courtesy of Willa Kim. Photo © Herbert
Migdoll.

Papillon

(left) Costume Design by Willa Kim for Richard Fein and Nancy Rodriguez, 1979. Choreography by Eliot Feld for The Feld Ballet. Courtesy of Willa Kim. Photo © Herbert Migdoll.

Papillon

(right) Costume Design by Willa Kim for Christine Sarry, 1979. Choreography by Eliot Feld for The Feld Ballet. Courtesy of Willa Kim. Photo © Herbert Migdoll.

ballets. Among their early successes was the premiere of *A Footstep of Air*, which opened on March 12, 1977, at the New York City Center. Writing in the *New York Times* (March 14, 1977), Clive Barnes observed: "The company dances this work like a jockey on a championship steed: all are splendid and look charming in their saucy Willa Kim costumes, which are stylizations of pleasant peasants."

While collaborating with Eliot Feld, Willa continued to design for other choreographers, including Glen Tetley and Michael Smuin. One of Tetley's most famous and often reproduced works, *Sphinx*, had its premiere by the American Ballet Theatre on December 9, 1977, at the Kennedy Center for the Performing Arts. The ballet, which is based on Jean Cocteau's examination of Oedipus, has since been performed by many other companies, always with Willa Kim's original designs and often under her direct supervision. These include the London Festival Ballet Company, Ater Balletó (Reggio Emilia, Italy), National Ballet of Canada, Den Morske Masjonal Ballet (Oslo), Dance Theatre of Harlem, Marodni Divadlo (Prague), and Ballet Florida.

Many of Willa Kim's most successful Broadway productions have been dance-based. They include *Dancin'*, which opened at the Broadhurst Theatre on March 27, 1978. The production was directed and choreographed by Bob Fosse, to music arranged and conducted by Gordon Lowry-Harrell. Though Miss Kim and Ann Reinking each earned Tony Award nominations for their work on *Dancin'*, it was Bob Fosse's choreography that won one of the two Tony Awards the production received at the 1978 Tony Award ceremonies. *Dancin'* would play 1,774 performances on Broadway before closing more than four years later.

The end of the 1970s found Willa Kim busier (if that was possible) than she was at the beginning of the decade. She designed costumes for John Guare's *Bosoms and Neglect* which was done originally at the Goodman in Chicago. It was becoming unusual for her to design a play without music or dancing. The play, directed by Mel Shapiro, and starring Marian Mercer as Deirdre, Kate Reid as Henny, and Paul Rudd as Scooper, opened in Chicago on

February 23, 1979, where it was warmly received. The subsequent transfer to the Longacre Theatre on Broadway on May 3, 1979, was less successful, and the show closed after only four performances.

The year 1979 also marked the fiftieth anniversary of the death of impresario Serge Diaghilev. The Joffrey Ballet and Rudolph Nureyev joined forces to present four ballets in commemoration, including *L'Après-midi d'un Faune*, *Petrouchka*, *Le Spectre de la Rose*, and *Parade*. Once again, Willa Kim supervised the reconstruction of Picasso's original designs, a labor of love in the middle of a busy schedule. *Homage to Diaghilev* debuted at the Mark Hellinger Theatre on March 7, 1979.

While she was working with Guare and Wulp on *Bosoms and Neglect* and supervising *Parade*, Miss Kim also was designing sets and costumes for Michael Smuin's *A Song for Dead Warriors*, a production by the San Francisco Ballet which opened at the War Memorial Opera House on May 17, 1979. For the ballet—which explores the taking of the American Indians' lands—Miss Kim designed giant bison as well as other costumes inspired by the clothing worn by several native peoples. *A Song for Dead Warriors* was a huge success, and both Smuin and Kim would win Emmy Awards when the ballet was broadcast on PBS' *Dance in America* in 1984.

In the summer of 1979, Miss Kim was again at work with Eliot Feld on his newest work, *Papillon*, which had its premiere on August 9, 1979, at the Lewiston (New York) ArtPark, with music by Jacques Offenbach performed by members of the Buffalo Philharmonic Orchestra.

This amazingly beautiful ballet, about the dangers to butterflies presented by nets and flames, included dancers costumed as chrysalises as well as adult butterflies. The ballet has remained in the repertoire of Feld's companies. The beauty of the dancing, costumes, and setting is invariably greeted enthusiastically by audiences and critics.

At the time of *Papillon's* premiere, Anna Kisselgoff wrote in the *New York Times* (August 12, 1979): "In this community of butterflies of all sizes and shapes—beautifully costumed by Willa Kim who did the spider-web set—Mr. Feld has created some of his best choreography in years. It is intensely classical but also quirky."

The model for *Papillon's* set, including the spider webs that an assistant created using macramé, hangs on one of the walls in Willa Kim's home. It has been placed carefully above a set of open shelves that are lined with containers and objects made of crystal. These objects catch the light that streams through the windows overlooking Broadway and refract color onto the scale model which is a perfect miniature of the *Papillon* set. When the light is just right, it provides a glimpse of the artistry Feld and Kim gave the ballet.

Willa Kim spent part of the last month of 1979 in Holland, where the Netherlands Dance Theatre was rehearsing a new piece by Czech choreographer Jiří Kylián, called *Dream Dances*. It premiered on December 7, 1979, in The Hague. After her husband, William Pène du Bois, returned to Europe in 1972, he always traveled to be with her whenever productions opened abroad. But at the end of 1979, not even the possibility of spending New Year's Eve with Billy in his beloved Paris could keep her from her drawing table in New York. Shortly before *Dream Dances* opened, she had been contacted by Michael Smuin about designing his newest ballet, which was to be based on Shakespeare's play, *The Tempest*.

Medusa

(top left) Costume Rendering by Willa Kim for Judith Jamison as "Medusa," 1978. Choreography by Margo Sappington for the Alvin Ailey Company. Courtesy of Willa Kim.

Medusa

(top right) Costume Rendering by Willa Kim for "Chorus Men," 1978. Choreography by Margo Sappington for the Alvin Ailey Company. Courtesy of Willa Kim.

Medusa

(bottom left) Costume Rendering by Willa Kim for "Chorus Women," 1978. Choreography by Margo Sappington for the Alvin Ailey Company. Courtesy of Willa Kim.

Medusa

Costume Rendering by Willa Kim for Clive Thompson as "Perseus," 1978. Choreography by Margo Sappington for the Alvin Ailey Company. Courtesy of Willa Kim.

Part Three • Ballets, Musicals, and Plays

Designing costumes for a full-length ballet, in particular for a new production like *The Tempest*, is time-consuming. There are meetings with other members of the production team, budgets to prepare, sources to identify, and designs to draw and paint. While exhaustive research can be both taxing and time-consuming—particularly for a production set in a certain time period or one with which the audience is quite familiar—it has always been a crucial part of the design process for Willa Kim. Her studio is filled with boxes of clippings from magazines, photocopies of works of art, pages torn from newspapers and advertisements, old postcards, and swatches of color from a variety of sources.

When she designs a production, Miss Kim gathers together useful books (which normally line her numerous shelves stretching from floor to ceiling) and stacks them on every available surface so that they are close to hand. Many of them will have pages marked, while others will be perused page-by-page as Miss Kim gathers her thoughts. Because of her deep research and her active participation in the creation of a production from its inception, she often understands the production as well or better than the director or choreographer.

Miss Kim can be tenacious about her ideas and designs and doesn't wait to be told what a costume or element of scenery looks like because she *knows*. She doesn't create conventional beauty and doesn't take the obvious choices, preferring to invent new ones. She has discovered numerous ways of expressing beauty, often through intricate details. Even when all the costumes in one of her productions are drab and colorless, their artistry and inherent wit make them beautiful.

While a Willa Kim production is almost immediately identifiable, it is often difficult to identify the exact source of inspiration. Her work is inspired by her research and collaboration with others working on a production, but at the same time it is strikingly original. For example her 1976 ballet, *Under the Sun*, was conceived as a tribute to Alexander Calder. The colors and geometric motifs recall Calder without being exactly like Calder. The many Asian-themed pieces she has designed, including *Le Rossignol* (1969, 1971), *Shinjū* (1975), and *Turandot* (2005), all evoke a particular time and place yet are clearly new visions of that time and place.

When Miss Kim completes a production, her reference books are returned to the shelves, and boxes containing manila envelopes full of research are carefully stored in clothes closets—her "research repositories." Throughout her career she has generally placed her original sketches in plastic sleeves to protect them while they are being used in costume work-rooms. Pieces of research relevant to the design may be placed in the sleeve behind the rendering along with fabric swatches. When the designs are put away after a production has opened, those research elements often remain in place where they can be useful for revivals.

Most of her ideas—whether an individual design element or a small measure of inspiration—are absorbed into the creative part of her brain and then circulated (often in surprising ways) back into the costumes and scenery she designs. Her designs are characterized by a distillation of research which is elaborated into an idea and then is finally transformed into a sketch. She keeps the visual material, the patterns of movement she has observed, and the musical themes she has heard, all circulating in her mind as she listens to her collaborators. When her ideas are fully formed, they emerge with a rush, and are quickly sketched and then painted on the white watercolor paper she generally uses.

Long-time collaborator Tony Walton suggested in an interview with Deborah Quilter in *Dance Spirit* (April 2000) that "Willa works more by osmosis—drifting about [the] studio, picking things up and feeling them…To someone who doesn't know her, she may not appear to be listening. But, in fact, she's tuning in totally and once she's hit upon them, her designs and intentions are absolutely clear."

When Ray Diffen began working almost exclusively for the Metropolitan Opera House designing and making costumes, it became increasingly difficult for him to maintain his costume house with the high standards he required. Ray Diffen Stage Clothes, Inc. closed in October 1979, which meant that some of the people employed in the costume work room had to find new work. Sally Ann Parsons, who specialized in dance costumes for Ray Diffen, was available when Willa Kim needed someone to create the costumes for *The Tempest*. She relocated to San Francisco while the costumes were being constructed along with some of her Diffen colleagues. Some new space had just been created for the San Francisco Opera and was converted, temporarily, into a costume workroom so that the costumes for *The Tempest* could be made.

Music for *The Tempest* was composed by Paul Chihara (after Henry Purcell) who had collaborated with Michael Smuin and Willa Kim on *Shinjū*. The sets were designed by Tony Walton. The ballet opened in the War Memorial Opera House in San Francisco on May 12, 1980, to rave reviews. It featured Attila Ficzere as Prospero, David McNaughton as Ariel, Tomm Ruud as Ferdinand, Horacio Cifuentes as Caliban, and Evelyn Cisneros as Miranda. *The Tempest* was broadcast by PBS on *Dance in America: "Live from the Opera House"* on April 5, 1981. Willa Kim received her first Emmy Award for this broadcast. Emmys were also awarded to Michael Smuin for his choreography and Paul Chihara for the music.

Not only did Willa Kim design costumes for *The Tempest* in 1980, she also designed two dances for Eliot Feld. *Circa* premiered at the Eastman Theatre in Rochester, New York, on May 29, 1980. On August 8, 1980, *Circa* was again performed at the Pepsico Summerfare Festival at the Performing Arts Center at the State University of New York in Purchase with another new Feld ballet receiving its world premiere: *Scenes for the Theatre*. Miss Kim designed both sets and costumes for *Scenes for the Theatre* which was choreographed to music by Aaron Copeland. Copeland joined Willa Kim and Eliot Feld on stage opening night with featured dancers John Sowinski, Nancy Thuesen, Gregory Mitchell, Mary Randolph, and Gloria Brisbin.

Willa Kim devoted the fall of 1980 to designing and supervising the construction of costumes for a new musical, *Sophisticated Ladies*, featuring the music of Duke Ellington. Many of the costumes were made by Grace Miceli and her sister, Maria Brizzi, of Grace Costumes Inc. Founded by the two sisters in 1961, Grace Costumes often made costumes from Miss Kim's designs.

Kim had painstakingly researched the designs for *Sophisticated Ladies*. She told an interviewer in the *New York Times* (September 20, 1981) that she had read "every book on

The Tempest

Costume Rendering Details by Willa Kim for Caliban, 1980. Choreography by Michael Smuin for San Francisco Ballet. Courtesy of Willa Kim.

The Tempest

Costume Design by Willa Kim for two dancers as the "Sea," 1980. Choreography by Michael Smuin for San Francisco Ballet. Courtesy of Willa Kim. Photo © Lloyd Englert.

The Tempest

Costume Rendering by Willa Kim for Antonio Lopez as "Trinculo," 1980. Choreography by Michael Smuin for San Francisco Ballet. Courtesy of Willa Kim.

The Tempest
Costume Rendering by Willa Kim for Horacio Cifuentes as "Caliban," 1980. Choreography by Michael Smuin for San Francisco Ballet. Courtesy of Willa Kim.

The Tempest
Costume Design by Willa Kim for David McNaughton as "Ariel," 1980. Choreography by Michael Smuin for San Francisco Ballet. Courtesy of Willa Kim.

The Tempest
Costume Rendering by Willa Kim for Robert Sund as "Bacchus," 1980. Choreography by Michael Smuin for San Francisco Ballet. Courtesy of Willa Kim.

Ellington, his own books, his son's books, I went to that museum on Seventh Avenue to research black history. I listened to the lyrics of the songs. Then I would think of what the performer had to do. In Phyllis Hyman's swing number, for example, I decided to give her a real showgirl's costumes, with a revealing feathered skirt and beaded top because the number was hot enough to support it and because she's six feet tall in her stocking feet and can carry it."

Much has been written about the difficulties *Sophisticated Ladies* had during its pre-Broadway tryout in Washington, D.C. It opened at the Kennedy Center on January 13, 1981, to mixed reviews, prompting the producers to delay the New York opening until March.

By the time it opened in New York, *Sophisticated Ladies* had gone through three directors and three choreographers. This translated into substantial changes which in turn meant using costumes for scenes other than the ones for which they had been designed. With an overall budget of $175,000 for the costumes this was a challenging task at best, and under the circumstances was even more difficult. Willa Kim later reported that when difficulties with the production first emerged, everything about the production was suspect and some of her costumes were taken out of the show. Watching the distortion from their intended use became increasingly uncomfortable, and when the possibility of traveling to Italy arose, she decided to go. Glen Tetley's 1977 ballet, *Sphinx*, complete with her original costume designs, was being added to the repertory of the Ater Balletó. The company was anxious to have her attend the opening at the Teatro Municipale Romolo Valli in Reggio Emilia, on January 18, 1981.

When Willa Kim returned from Italy, Tony Walton was eager to talk with her. Michael Smuin had been brought in as a replacement director and choreographer for *Sophisticated Ladies*, he reported, and she should travel to Washington as quickly as possible—Walton was headed back to D.C. on the next train. Miss Kim repacked her suitcase, returned to the airport, and flew to the nation's capitol. Not only had Michael Smuin restored her costume designs, he had transformed the entire production. He had even brought his friend, composer Paul Chihara, to assist with the musical arrangements.

Sophisticated Ladies opened on Broadway at the Lunt-Fontanne Theatre on March 1, 1981 to rave reviews for all the major performers, including Gregory Hines, Judith Jameson, Phyllis Hyman, Hinton Battle, and

Sphinx
Costume Design by Willa Kim for Martine Van Hamel, 1977. Choreographed by Glen Tetley for American Ballet Theatre. Courtesy of Willa Kim. Photo © Martha Swope.

Gregg Burge. Enthusiastic reviews also greeted the costumes. *New York Times* drama critic Frank Rich wrote that "Miss Kim's costumes are so profuse and brightly hued that they transform the cast into an ever-changing satin rainbow. That's just how it should be." (NYT March 2, 1981)

Willa Kim won a Tony Award for the costumes for *Sophisticated Ladies*. Altogether the musical received nine Tony Award nominations and played for nearly two years—rather remarkable for a production that almost didn't make it to Broadway.

Later that fall, Willa Kim designed costumes for David Henry Hwang's *Family Devotions*, which opened on October 18, 1981, at the Public Theatre. She also designed costumes for *The Wild Boy* which had its world premiere on December 12, 1981. American Ballet Theatre had commissioned Sir Kenneth MacMillan to choreograph *The Wild Boy* with Mikhail Baryshnikov dancing the title role at the Kennedy Center premiere. The original company included Natalia Markarova, Kevin McKenzie, and Robert La Fosse. American Ballet Theatre added *The Wild Boy* to its New York repertory on April 19, 1982, at the Metropolitan Opera House with Robert La Fosse in the title role.

Early in 1982, Willa Kim returned to the American Place Theatre to design John Guare's new play, *Lydie Breeze*. Directed by Louis Malle, it opened on February 25, 1982. She then turned to designs for a series of new dance pieces, among them *Stravinsky Piano Pieces* by Michael Smuin, which the San Francisco Ballet opened at the War Memorial Auditorium on April 6, 1982.

A costume designer seldom makes a grand entrance at a premiere the way actors do. But that is exactly what happened for Willa Kim on the night of June 1, 1982, when the Joyce Theatre celebrated its opening. Willa Kim entered with other dance-world celebrities under the brightly lit marquee at the corner of Eighth Avenue and 19th Street in the Chelsea neighborhood of New York City. Mikhail Baryshnikov, Michael Bennett, Alexandra Danilova, Louis Falco, Eliot Feld, and Cora Cahan, executive director for the Feld Ballet, were among those in the audience when the refurbished Elgin Theatre was dedicated as a new performance space specifically devoted to dance.

Two days later, on June 3, 1982, Eliot Feld's company, then known as the Feld Ballet, began a four-week-long season in the Joyce Theatre, its new home. During the evening, *Over the Pavement* had its world premiere, and *A Footstep of Air* (1977) was revived. Both featured costumes by Willa Kim. *Over the Pavement* used the back wall of the theatre as background for the seven male dancers that Willa Kim costumed in stained and much-used work clothes. *A Footstep of Air* was performed by most of the company, including Eliot Feld himself, to selected Irish and Scottish folk songs arranged by Ludwig von Beethoven. The costumes, using the original designs, are among Willa Kim's most witty creations, featuring elements of Scottish and Irish national dress. Many of the costume pieces are enhanced by one of her signature design elements, painted colors and textures. What appear to be tweed leggings are painted designs rather than actual woven fabric. Bold plaids are also intermingled with knitted pieces representing the Aran Isles.

During the next four weeks, additional dances were premiered and others revived. Among those that Kim and Feld did together were *Half Time* (1978), *Danzon Cubano* (1978), *La Vida* (1978), and *Scenes* (originally titled *Scenes for the Theatre*, 1980).

Just as when their collaborations first began, the reviews were unanimous in their praise, echoing the common thinking that Feld and Kim were uniquely paired. Their close relationship and collaborations continued into the mid-1980s with other new works (and continued revivals of others) among them *Summer's Lease* and *Three Dances* in 1983, and *The Jig Is Up*, *Adieu*, and *The Real McCoy* in 1984.

The costume designs for *The Jig Is Up* are raggedy and tattered layers, convenient and somewhat stylish, appropriate for movement by dancers following a pied piper through a series of songs written and performed by the Bothy Band, Archibald McDonald, and John

Sophisticated Ladies
    Costume Rendering (Sketch # 2, dated 1980) by Willa Kim for Judith Jamison in "Jubliee Stomp," 1981. Courtesy of Willa Kim.

Sophisticated Ladies
    Costume Rendering (Sketch # B, dated 1980) by Willa Kim for Beth Bowles in "Echoes of Harlem," 1981. Courtesy of Willa Kim.

Song & Dance
Costume Rendering, Sketch # 24, by Willa Kim for Cynthia Onrubia, 1985. Courtesy of Willa Kim.

Song & Dance
Costume Rendering, SK#26, by Willa Kim for Charlotte d'Amboise, 1985. Courtesy of Willa Kim.

Cunningham. The costumes include some appliqués of texture contrasts that are sometimes smooth and shiny and sometimes textured. The budget for the production was not big enough to have the costumes made so Eliot Feld and Cora Cahan informed Miss Kim that it would have to be "shopped." She was, however, provided with a driver who took her to numerous stores. When she returned to the theatre, she began disassembling the garments and handing new combinations of pieces to Sally Ann Parsons who stitched them back together. The resulting "collage" was a creative solution that became even more remarkable when small segments of the remaining sleeves, legs, and skirts were appliquéd on to the "new" garments. *The Jig Is Up* debuted on April 10, 1984, at the Joyce Theatre.

Adieu had its premiere four days after the debut of *The Jig Is Up*. A large black robe was central to the dance. It was initially worn by Donlin Foreman and, being voluminous, it concealed other dancers beneath it. During the dance it was used as a privacy screen, a blanket, and as part of a whirlwind. Eliot Feld later reflected on the ballet, in an interview in the in-flight magazine of Korean Air, *Morning Calm* (November 1990), saying: "Frequently, Willa will design something that rather shocks me, but then it turns out to be an extraordinary addition to the ballet and to its images." He continued, "For instance, in *Adieu*—I had no idea of it as an abstract work as it worked out, and I think it turned out to be of poetic images and a major contribution to the ballet."

The final new ballet that season, celebrating the company's tenth anniversary, was *The Real McCoy*, choreographed by Eliot Feld to music by Cole Porter. *New York Times* dance critic Jennifer Dunning wrote (May 1, 1984) that "there was a collective sigh from the audience as the curtain went up on the cool, airy space that Mr. Fisher, the lighting designer, has created for a man, a woman, four chorus boys and a ballet, a gaggle of white canes and a magnificent silver chaise lounge to move through. And Miss Kim has given us the ultimate in chic light casuals for the man, a sexy pink cap and dress, spangled and feathered for the woman, and silvery suits for the chorus."

Eliot Feld and Willa Kim would continue to collaborate, but this series of ballets in 1984 illustrates their extraordinary artistic compatibility. Each possesses a strong vision of the way dancers move and how their forms should be enhanced. Each has an appreciation for the other's artistic vision. Thus it is not surprising that they make excellent (though often strong-willed) colleagues. Miss Kim would later observe that among her best designs were some of her early ballets for Feld, as well as the ones from the mid-1980s, including *The Jig Is Up*.

In 1983, Willa Kim received an achievement award, honoring her Korean heritage, from the National Association of Asian-American Professional Women, a New York-based organization. Three women were honored for their accomplishments. Along with Miss Kim, Michiko Kakutani, head critic of the *New York Times Review of Books*, and New York television anchor Kaity Tong, received the 1983 Asian Woman of Achievement Award.

While she was designing the series of new ballets for Feld and supervising the revival of others, Willa Kim was also busy designing other productions. The York Theatre Company wanted her to design costumes for *Elizabeth and Essex*, John Curry was planning a series of dances on ice for his company, and the possibility of a new Broadway musical based on Charlie Chaplin was in the planning stages on the West Coast. To help with all these projects, she needed an assistant. John David Ridge had worked with her on several productions. She knew he was busy but contacted him anyway. He urged her to consider Richard Schurkamp, a colleague Ridge had known at Brooks Costume Company, and she did.

Willa Kim flew back to Los Angeles to meet with Michael Smuin about the musical *Chaplin*. By early spring 1983 *Chaplin* had been cast and the costumes were being made, but many details still needed to be worked out. The musical had not been written to be performed in chronological order which meant numerous changes of scenery and costumes, and some difficulty in keeping the characters straight as they moved through time.

The musical was written by and starring Anthony Newley (1931-1999) with co-writer Stanley Ralph Ross. It opened at the Dorothy Chandler Pavilion on August 12, 1983. The reviews were not very good which put the planned November 10, 1983, opening at the Mark Hellinger Theatre in New York in jeopardy.

Leslie Bricusse, with whom Anthony Newley had collaborated on *Stop the World, I Want to Get Off* and other musicals was brought in. Musical numbers and scenes were rewritten, the show was restructured to give it a more logical time progression, audiences became increasingly receptive, and the Los Angeles critics were invited back. Their reviews were more enthusiastic, and plans to move the show to Broadway resumed. But money difficulties, caused in part by small audiences and major rewrites, brought those plans to an end.

The costumes were successful, however, as was the new relationship between Willa Kim and Richard Schurkamp. He had gone to her apartment for an interview, but ended up being put to work immediately. Schurkamp remains one of Miss Kim's most devoted assistants and admirers, having worked with her on *Song & Dance* (1985), *Victor/Victoria* (1995), and *The Bay at Nice* (2004) among dozens of musicals and ballets.

An experienced assistant for a variety of designers, Schurkamp suggests that Miss Kim doesn't work like anyone else, mainly because she refuses to compromise. He also says that because Willa Kim's costume designs are not traditional dressmaker's sketches, but rather the kind an artist creates, they can be misinterpreted. As her assistant, he helps costume makers understand what she is after.

What might look initially like a squiggly line on one of Miss Kim's costume renderings can in fact be an important element of the design. Every line must be understood and then transformed into fabric and color before it becomes apparent that the squiggly line wasn't a mistake or a casual line. Once complete (and successfully interpreted) a costume can be held next to the rendering and the intention becomes even clearer. Willa Kim has been known to ask for costumes to be made over again, moving a line, an appliqué, or a splash of color one way or the other by what appears to be a slight degree.

Judy Adamson, a long-time draper at Barbara Matera Ltd., recalls making a series of costumes for a Feld ballet. She says that "it seemed as if Willa was torturing the painter, asking for some spots to be moved a half inch this way and others a half inch another direction." Adamson continues: "No one quite understood why the position of those spots was so important until the costumes were together on stage in the musical number for which they were made, and suddenly their relative positions made sense. They were in exactly the right place on a group of dancers who were different heights."

Willa Kim states this ability in another way, suggesting that she is lucky enough to have a kind of "perfect pitch" when it comes to color and shape. She is able cut a piece of trim the exact size needed on a costume, and to mix an exact color. Her instinct is uncanny—and unfailing. She can tell one piece of black spandex from another piece of black spandex, dyed at different times, as shoppers in the New York costume houses will readily testify.

Willa Kim's ability to interpret movement in costumes she designed and to approach the art of costume design like the art of painting was especially useful for her next projects, including *Jamboree*, with choreography by Gerald Arpino. The dance, a celebration of all things Texan, was commissioned by the city of San Antonio and debuted in the Lila Cockrell Theatre in San Antonio on June 20, 1984. This world premiere was followed on November 21, 1984, by another one, when *Odalisque*, with choreography by Glen Tetley, opened at the O'Keefe Centre for the Performing Arts in Toronto. The ballet was commissioned by the National Ballet of Canada as part of their 25th Anniversary Celebration of the National Ballet of Canada School.

Miss Kim also returned to designing costumes for ice skaters, with three pieces—*Moon Skate*, *Presto Barbaro*, and *Butterfly*—for John Curry and his company of skaters. Curry,

HoTsy ToTsy ReinDeer DANCE"

CIGARETTE GIRL

who won the Olympic Gold Medal for Great Britain in 1976 in men's figure skating formed the John Curry Skating Company in 1977 as a way to showcase the artistry of ice skaters. For the 1984 tour, he concentrated on training his company of ice skaters in ballet techniques and turning them into ice dancers. Most of the pieces in the repertory that opened on July 26, 1984, at the Metropolitan Opera House were choreographed by modern dance choreographers, including Twyla Tharp, Lar Lubovitch, Peter Martins, Laura Dean and Eliot Feld. (John Curry contributed some pieces himself.) The reviews were splendid, complimenting the artistry of the dances and of the skaters, as well as the use of the Metropolitan Opera House as a respite from the sweltering New York summer.

Butterfly, set to Puccini's music, was a solo piece for Dorothy Hamill, the American Olympic Gold Medal winner, who appeared as a guest artist. Both *Butterfly* and *Presto Barbaro*, using music by Leonard Bernstein, were choreographed by John Curry. *Moon Skate* was choreographed by Eliot Feld. Dance critic Anna Kisselgoff, wrote in the *New York Times* (July 28, 1984) that "Mr. Feld's 'Moon Skate,' a solo for Mr. Curry set to the slow movement of Ravel's G Major Concerto, is one of the best things Mr. Feld has choreographed in any medium." She also noted that "Willa Kim has designed a fabulous costume for Mr. Curry—a loose shirt with a vestlike motif and pants that balloon out as he moves." It was clear that joining Feld and Kim with Curry's artistry on ice was a success. The following summer Willa Kim would design costumes for

Legs Diamond
Costume Rendering by Willa Kim for Carol Ann Baxter, Colleen Dunn, Deanna Dys, Gwen Miller, and Wendy Waring for the Hotsy Totsy Club "Reindeer Dance," 1988. Courtesy of Willa Kim.

Legs Diamond
Costume Rendering by Willa Kim for Deanna Dys as "Hotsy Totsy Cigarette Girl," 1988. Courtesy of Willa Kim.

Legs Diamond
Costume Rendering by
Willa Kim for Julie
Wilson as "Flo" for the
"Man Nobody Could
Love," 1988. Courtesy
of Willa Kim.

HEAVY SILK
CHARMEUSE

SILVER LAME

BLACK SILK VELVET

SK 29
FLO JULIE WILSON
"THE MAN NOBODY COULD LOVE"

aug 1988

SK # 15

FLO: JULIE WILSON
1st DRESS FOR
HOTSY TOTSY CLUB

"LEGS DIAMOND"

JUNE 1988

Legs Diamond
Costume Rendering by
Willa Kim for Julie Wilson
as "Flo," "1st dress for
Hotsy Totsy," 1988.
Courtesy of Willa Kim.

SILVER & BLACK
LAME

VELVET

BLACK VELVET

BUTTON - BLACK FUR.

SHIRRED

SK 28
FUNERAL
FLO
JULIE WILSON

"LEGS DIAMOND"

Legs Diamond
Costume Rendering by Willa Kim for Julie Wilson "Flo" for the Funeral
Scene, 1988. Courtesy of Willa Kim.

Curry's company once again, for *Mishima* and *Spartacus*, both of which opened on August 8, 1985, at the Kennedy Center.

The spring of 1985 was busy with the creation of costume designs for *Against the Sky*, a ballet for Eliot Feld that opened on April 3, 1985, with his company of dancers in repertory at the Joyce Theatre. On April 15th another Feld ballet, *Impromptu*, was revived and performed by Karen Kain of the National Ballet of Canada, who joined the company as a guest artist for the season. With music by Johannes Brahms, *Impromptu* was originally performed by Birgit Keil (prima ballerina of the Stuttgart Ballet) on October 19, 1976, at the New York Public Theatre's Newman Theatre.

Most of Miss Kim's time and creative energy that spring and summer, however, was devoted to creating costume designs for a new Broadway musical, *Song & Dance*. She had new collaborators for this musical, including Andrew Lloyd Webber (music), Don Black (lyrics), Richard Maltby, Jr. (director) and Peter Martins (choreographer). Robin Wagner, with whom she had collaborated in 1972 on *Lysistrata*, designed the scenery and Jules Fisher, a colleague on numerous productions, created the lights. *Song & Dance* opened on September 18, 1985 at the Royale Theatre, starring Bernadette Peters (who won a Tony Award for her performance) as a hat maker who immigrated to New York from England, and Christopher d'Amboise as one of her suitors. The reviews were not very positive, but the musical was popular with audiences and ran for over a year before closing on November 8, 1986.

The following spring when the Tony Award nominations were announced, *Song & Dance* received a total of eight nominations, including one for Willa Kim's costume designs, her fourth.

Miss Kim has been quoted as saying that she reached a point in her career in the mid-1980s when she felt more challenged designing plays than ballets because the sustained plots that develop characters in plays presented a greater challenge. She has also been quoted as saying that she loves to design short ballet pieces because they challenge her to express much in a short time. The conflict between these two statements can be resolved by understanding that she is always looking for new ways to both design and realize costumes. Her curiosity has not diminished throughout her career, nor has her desire to be challenged. Her choice of projects and designs for those projects is never monotonous.

In 1986, she designed two plays that presented unique challenges, Eugene O'Neill's *Long Day's Journey into Night* and *The Front Page* by Ben Hecht and Charles MacArthur. *Long Day's Journey into Night* reunited Willa Kim with the director Jonathan Miller with whom she had worked on *The Old Glory* back in 1964. The play, starring Jack Lemmon as James Tyrone, and Peter Gallagher and Kevin Spacey as his sons, opened at the Broadhurst Theatre on April 28, 1986. Miss Kim's costumes successfully evoked a Connecticut summer in 1912, and her designs for Bethel Leslie's Mary Tyrone were especially beautiful and sad.

In contrast, *The Front Page* was both beautiful and buoyant. Directed by Jerry Zaks, it opened on November 23, 1986, at the Vivian Beaumont Theatre. John Lithgow starred as the formidable managing editor Walter Burns and Richard Thomas played crack newspaper reporter Hildy Johnson, who was trying to exchange writing for a rag for a respectable career. Wearing suitable 1930s attire and a mustache, Thomas faced down a dowager mother-in-law-to-be, played by Beverly May, and tried to placate his bride-to-be, played by Julie Hagerty. The show was wildly successful for all involved, including Tony Walton, who designed the set, an appropriately seedy newsroom in a Chicago courthouse.

Willa Kim's costumes for *The Front Page* were well received. *Time* magazine commented (December 8, 1986) that Miss Kim's costumes "evoke the era without prettifying it." Robert Brustein in the *New Republic* (January 5, 1987) wrote at length about his admiration for the entire production, including "Jerome Dempsey as the rotund, orotund mayor, equipped (by the costumer Willa Kim, whose period designs are characterizations in themselves) with tailcoat and fez."

Between these two plays were additional premieres with Eliot Feld, including *Echo*, *Skara Brae*, and *Bent Planes*. These new ballets were part of The Feld Ballet's fall season at the Joyce Theatre. Shortly before *The Front Page* opened, Willa Kim also designed costumes for *Sentimental Reasons*, choreographed by Michael Smuin for Cynthia Gregory. The long-time principal dancer with the American Ballet Theatre had formed her own company in 1986, which was launched with a *Celebration Tour* at the Lehman Center at Lehman College in New York, on September 20, 1986.

The following year presented new challenges, among them designs for television and film. It would be surprising if a designer with Miss Kim's breadth of credits were not offered opportunities to design major motion pictures, especially considering the time she spent early in her career at Paramount Studios. However, designing

Regina Wine Vinegar
Commercial
(left) Costume Rendering by
Willa Kim. Romaine Lettuce
Ensemble, 1989. Courtesy of
Willa Kim.

Regina Wine Vinegar
Commercial
(below) Costume Rendering
by Willa Kim. Potato Salad
Ensemble, 1989. Courtesy of
Willa Kim.

Regina Wine Vinegar
Commercial
Costume Rendering by
Willa Kim. Garden Salad
Ensemble, 1989. Courtesy
of Willa Kim.

Regina Wine Vinegar Commercial
Costume Design by Willa Kim. Garden Salad detail, 1989. Courtesy of Willa Kim.
Courtesy of *Theatre Crafts*, March 1989, "Designers On Design: Willa Kim" by Beth
Howard. Photo © Donnelly Marks.

Kore

Costume Design by Willa Kim for Buffy Miller, 1988. Choreography by Eliot Feld for The Feld Ballet. Courtesy of Willa Kim. Photo © Lois Greenfield.

Asia

Costume Design by Willa Kim for Lynn Aaron and Darren Gibson, 1989. Choreography by Eliot Feld for The Feld Ballet. Courtesy of Willa Kim. Photo © Lois Greenfield.

movies involves spending considerable time on location and the film possibilities presented to her never were convenient in her schedule. She did, however, contribute some costume designs to Francis Ford Coppola's *Gardens of Stone*. The movie, starring James Caan and Laurence Fishburne, was released in 1987. Willa Kim received credit for the costume designs with Judianna Makovsky.

Willa Kim also designed the costumes worn by Julie Andrews on her hour-long holiday television special, *Julie Andrews: The Sound of Christmas*. First broadcast by the ABC Television Network on December 16, 1987, it was filmed on location in and around Salzburg, Austria. Both Julie Andrews and Willa Kim delighted in the locations used for the special, which took them to churches, palaces, gardens, and museums where the splendor of the Baroque was apparent. Miss Kim later observed that she did not appreciate Baroque art until experiencing it during that trip.

Between these two filmed productions, Willa Kim designed *A Dance for Two* for the fall season of the Feld Ballet at the Joyce Theatre. The ballet, created for its two performers, Lynn Aaron and Darren Gibson, opened on September 28, 1987. Miss Kim re-designed *Echo* (1986) specifically for Karen Kain, guest artist with the Feld company from the National Ballet of Canada. Jack Anderson wrote in the *New York Times* (October 4, 1987) that "Mr. Feld has created a dance that could have been performed at a feast in a story from the 'Arabian Nights.' And Willa Kim has costumed Ms. Kain to resemble an odalisque."

As early as the opening of *The Front Page* in 1986, Willa Kim was working on a projected Broadway musical with Peter Allen and Harvey Fierstein, based on a Warner Brothers movie called *The Rise and Fall of Legs Diamond*. The movie, released in 1960 starring Ray Danton and Warren Oates, was an entertaining gangster film about jewel thieves in Depression-era New York. In 1988, the theatre production finally made it to the "Great White Way." Directed by Robert Alan Ackerman, *Legs Diamond* starred Peter Allen, who also wrote the music and lyrics. It opened on December 26, 1988, at the Mark Hellinger Theatre. The reviews were poor, although Miss Kim's costumes were applauded for creating clever 1930s-era showgirls who danced to Alan Johnson's choreography in the Hotsy Totsy Club. Her glamorous gowns for Julie Wilson who played Flo, the manager of the speakeasy, were also admired. When the Tony Award nominations were announced late the following spring, Julie Wilson, Alan Johnson, and Willa Kim were included.

Shortly after *Legs Diamond* opened, Willa Kim was approached by Lowe Marschalk/ New York, an advertising agency with the account for RJR Nabisco Brands, Inc. Patricia Sutula and Scott Sorokin at Lowe Marschalk had the idea to promote Regina Wine Vinegar as the perfect accompaniment to any salad. Their idea was to display salads on a high fashion runway, with the caption: "Because it's made from 100% California wine, Regina can dress up the taste of any salad."

Willa Kim created ensembles for four high-fashion models dressed as salads: a Garden Salad ensemble, a Pasta Salad ensemble, a Potato salad ensemble, and a Romaine Lettuce ensemble. The garments, including a bustier made from asparagus tips, radish earrings, a lettuce coat, red onion necklaces, spiral pasta sleeve caps, beaded tomatoes festooning skirts, saucy hats made of mushrooms and garlic, and slices of cucumber finishing necklines, were examples of "what the best-dressed salads are wearing."

The thirty-second advertising spot was telecast at half-time of the Rose Bowl Football game on New Year's Day in 1989, and was an enormous hit. The salad costumes attracted attention from other ad agencies and television audiences. Once the filming of commercials is complete the costumes used in them are generally discarded or sold. But while the series of "takes" were being filmed, Willa Kim called Harold Koda, then costume curator of the Edward C. Blum Design Laboratory of the Fashion Institute of Technology. He raved about their couture quality and as a result, Miss Kim convinced RJR Nabisco Brands and Lowe Marshalk, Inc. to donate them to the F.I.T. collection.

The four costumes were made at Barbara Matera, Ltd., in a dazzling display of beading and texture bravura. The details, designed by Willa Kim and created under Barbara Matera's personal direction, were all exceedingly well done, from the deviled eggs and olives in the garden salad to the potato slices and scallions in the potato salad. The back of the romaine lettuce coat is a perfect replica of the color of lettuce as it deepens from the center of the spine to the edge of the leaves.

While Barbara Matera (1929-2001) did not often make costumes from Willa Kim's designs, the collaborations between them were notable, including the four salad costumes and one of Miss Kim's early designs for the Santa Fe Opera, *The Magic Flute* (1968). Coincidentally both collaborations included witty uses of food. Papagena, after her disguise as an old crone is removed, wears a skirt trimmed with fruits and vegetables.

The very successful 1989 spring season of the Feld Ballet was a fitting second act to a year that began with Willa Kim's adventure with television commercials. The Feld Ballet's spring season at the Joyce Theatre included three world premieres and two New York debuts, all with choreography by Eliot Feld and costume designs by Willa Kim. Their collaborations would continue, but this particular season was memorable for its striking originality. Shortly after the new ballets were added to the repertory, Eliot Feld said that "If I had to find one word that characterizes her designs it would be 'invention.'" (*Theatre Crafts*, March 1989) The Feld Ballet's 1989 season featured lighting design by Allen Lee Hughes, a successful new addition to their team.

Two of the new Feld pieces, *Kore* and *Love Song Waltzes* were performed on February 4, 1989. *Kore*, a solo performed by Buffy Miller as the goddess Persephone to music by Steve Reich, had its world premiere on July 15, 1988, at the Teatro ai Parchi, in Nervi, Italy. *Love Song Waltzes* was performed for the first time that night, and was a major addition to Feld's repertory. Danced by four couples who often changed partners, the ballet was a stunning success. Anna Kisselgoff in the *New York Times* (February 7 1989) wrote, "Willa Kim's costumes among her best, are satin gowns of different colors while the men are in stylized frock coats. The sense of period is indistinct, the dynamics are contemporary."

Asia was the next new piece, performed on February 8, 1989, choreographed to Ravel's *Shéhérazade* by Feld for five women and one man, Darren Gibson. Anna Kisselgoff was impressed by the variety of interpretations possible within the piece, writing in the *New York Times* (February 10, 1989) that "Willa Kim's costumes are luscious, with just enough glitz to remind us that 'Asia' is not a harem ballet of yore."

Shadow's Breath, a duet for Jeffrey Neeck and Lynn Aaron had its world premiere in Philadelphia on February 27, 1988. When it was performed in New York on February 18, 1989, Anna Kisselgoff wrote: "Miss Aaron comes fully into her own here, dancing with a daring that is only partly related to the technical difficulties of the choreography. She is dressed in a striking ruffled gray-blue tunic by Willa Kim that suggests one shoulder is bare, and she is caught initially in the icy glow of Allen Lee Hughes's lighting against a black background." (NYT February 20, 1989). The music was Mozart's Rondo in A Minor, and although the piece was only eleven minutes long, it represented much of Feld's and Kim's combined artistry in the display of movement.

Adding a "rap musical" to her extensive list of credits might seem unusual, but Willa Kim always embraces new challenges. Miss Kim also keeps commitments made to old friends and former collaborators, such as John Wulp and Patricia Birch. Wulp had approached her about designing costumes for a new musical written by one of his former students, Randy Weiner, who studied with him at Playwrights Horizons Theatre School. *Club XII*, based on Shakespeare's *Twelfth Night*, was adapted by Rob Hanning and Randy Weiner. It opened at the WestBeth Theatre Center on December 8, 1990, conceived as a workshop with sets and costumes in place to garner interest in a full commercial production from theatre and movie producers. John Wulp produced and Patricia Birch—who had earlier appeared as a dancer in ballets designed by Willa Kim—was the director.

Willa Kim has lived on the upper West Side of Manhattan since 1968 and the WestBeth Theatre Center is all the way downtown, on Bank Street near the West Side Highway. Shopping for costumes and fabrics appropriate for rappers took Miss Kim away from her usual shops, restaurants and activities. She was so busy that returning calls and responding to messages was difficult. Until the show opened, Miss Kim was not available, even when it was Tommy Tune who was anxious to get in touch with her.

Part Four • Honors and Accolades

Tommy Tune had an idea for a Broadway musical based on the American folk hero, Will Rogers, that he thought was so compelling that it had to be done immediately. It didn't matter to him that his preferred set designer, Tony Walton. was on location with a movie in Hollywood. And it seemed irrelevant that his chosen costume designer, Willa Kim, was designing *Club XII* and had agreed to create costumes for some new ballets for Eliot Feld. Lighting designer Jules Fisher and Tommy Tune had both just won Tony Awards for *Grand Hotel*, but Fisher was involved with other projects. Tune didn't care that Jeff Calhoun was too involved with other productions in Los Angeles to sign on as an assistant choreographer. Tommy Tune was convinced that Peter Stone would write the story, Betty Comden and Adolph Green would be available to contribute the lyrics and that Cy Coleman would compose the music—if only these busy people would just listen to what he wanted to do!

The Will Rogers Follies
Costume Rendering (Sketch # 58) for Colleen Dunn as "Indian Princess," 1991. Courtesy of Willa Kim.

As it turned out, most of the schedules could be rearranged, except for Tony Walton's. The filming timetable for *Regarding Henry*, starring Harrison Ford and Annette Bening, would not allow Walton to travel from California to New York even for a brief time. So Tommy Tune simply arranged for plane tickets to the West Coast and for hotel rooms in Beverly Hills for everyone else. Tommy Tune's musical concept would prove to be valid. What developed into *The Will Rogers Follies* would happen very quickly for a full-scale Broadway musical—although not quite as quickly as Tune had hoped.

The Will Rogers Follies
Costume Rendering (Sketch #56) for Wendy Waring as "Indian Princess,"
1991. Courtesy of Willa Kim.

✦   *Part Four • Honors and Accolades*

Tommy Tune, Willa Kim, Jules Fisher, and Jeff Calhoun stayed at the Hollywood Roosevelt Hotel and Tony Walton joined them as often as possible during November 1990. During that month, Tommy Tune laid out for them his idea for the musical. They sat around the hotel pool, kicked around ideas, and sketched out some initial designs. They watched the 1952 movie, *The Story of Will Rogers* starring Eddie Cantor, as well as some other movies of that era. Mostly they just talked and talked until they had the production worked out, to their mutual satisfaction.

Tune had hoped that the musical would open in February. This proved to be impossible, but when *The Will Rogers Follies* did open at the Palace Theatre on May 1, 1991, it was everything that Tommy Tune promised it would be—and more. The reviews were wonderful—if somewhat quizzical about how Tune and his team had turned the folk hero Will Rogers into a song and dance man. Keith Carradine played the title role, supported by Cady Huffman, Dee Hoty, and Dick Latessa, in a multi-million dollar Broadway musical that paid homage to the Ziegfeld Follies of earlier Broadway eras. Miss Kim's experience assisting Raoul Pène du Bois on the *Ziegfeld Follies of 1957* had proven useful. Frank Rich wrote a lengthy review in the *New York Times* (May 2, 1991), commenting about a "Technicolor parade of Willa Kim costumes and Tony Walton sets that not only exceed these designers' remarkable past achievements, but in all likelihood top the living tableaux that Joseph Urban once concocted for Florenz Ziegfeld himself." Rich continued, saying that Miss Kim's costumes were "breathtaking, with such minor details as the lining of a 10-gallon hat and the intricately stitched pattern of a pair of suspenders capturing the designer's full imaginative attention."

With previews, *The Will Rogers Follies* ran for over one thousand performances. Nominated for eleven Tony Awards, the show won six: best musical, best original score, and two for Tommy Tune as director and choreographer. Jules Fisher won the award for lighting design, and Willa Kim won her second Tony Award, for her costume designs.

Once again, Willa Kim's legendary attention to design detail had paid off, especially concerning color and placement of decorative details. "Lighting designers know my wrath," Kim admitted in an interview in *Theatre Crafts* (March 1989). "To work on color and detail to the extent that I do, and drive the costume shop crazy and not okay something because it isn't the exact color, and then to see it onstage and everything looks brown—it makes me absolutely insane. I drove them crazy getting the right blue, the right fuchsia, and I didn't do that just because I'm sadistic," she continued. "I want to see the colors onstage. I meant them to be seen exactly as that."

Everyone who comes into contact with Willa Kim quickly realizes that she is not only very smart, but also very curious. Her curiosity extends from the process of design to the procedures used in making the costumes as well. Because she feels so much at home in costume

The Will Rogers Follies
Costume Rendering (Sketch #59) for Tonia Lynn as "Indian Princess," 1991. Courtesy of Willa Kim.

shops, she likes to spend as much time as possible in them when a show is in production, watching the garments being draped and made, dyed, and painted. She can be meticulous about having a costume made to look exactly like she drew it, but she can also take advantage of the "happy accidents" that can occur during the process. If she is in a workroom and something catches her eye, she can take advantage of new combinations of color or textures, and often suggests to a draper that she would prefer to "go with that!"

Willa Kim's relationship with Tommy Tune is a special one. Originally from Houston, Texas, Tune began to take dancing lessons at the age of five. In high school in Houston and during his college years at the University of Texas in Austin, he appeared in and choreographed musicals. After graduation he moved to New York, where his six-and-a-half-foot height proved to be an asset in early appearances on Broadway, beginning with *Baker Street* in 1965. Before *The Will Rogers Follies* he had done several Broadway shows, both as a performer and as a choreographer, each of them more successful than the last. He had worked with many designers. But in 1988 when he needed a special outfit for a benefit concert at the Hollywood Bowl, he approached Miss Kim about designing a costume for him. *Broadway at the Bowl* was an all-star benefit for the Music Center Opera Company, to be directed and choreographed by Jeff Calhoun.

Following her usual method, Miss Kim asked to see what he planned to do before agreeing. Tommy Tune later talked with Beth Howard for "Designers on Design: Willa Kim," an article that appeared in the March 1989 issue of *Theatre Crafts*. "I went to the middle of the room and she started drawing. She said, 'What do you want to accomplish with the number, and what do you want it to suggest, and where are you coming from, and where are you going, and what happened right before you stepped onstage?'—all these intelligent questions. And of course she understands dance. She takes turns where there's not a bend in the road and never veers from the center line. She's a paradox."

When Tommy Tune contacted Willa Kim about working on *The Will Rogers Follies*, she was already at work on costumes for Eliot Feld's new ballets. Feld included nine ballets in the repertory that his company (then known as Feld Ballets/New York) would perform during the 1991 fall season. Six of these, including three premieres, were designed by Willa Kim. Three of the dances—*Evoe*, *Clave*, and *Endsong*—had previews in New York City on August 9, 1991.

In an article in *The New York Times* (August 9, 1991) about the new Feld works, dance critic Jennifer Dunning examined Willa Kim and Eliot Feld's creative partnership. Dunning recounts an incident in which Miss Kim, in response to Mr. Feld's request for his dancers to look like clouds in the night sky, provided a set of sketches painted in shades of gray—the actual color of clouds at night. Feld countered with a request for more color in the clouds. "So it was back to the drawing board," wrote Dunning. "And Ms. Kim came up with what she laughingly refers to as conceptual costumes, with colored bits of different fabrics appliquéd to the bodice and skirts to give them a shimmering look. 'The top is the night sky, the bottom is the earth, and the arms are clouds,' Ms. Kim said, a hint of cheerful resignation in her voice. 'It's a saga.'"

The very real give-and-take in their relationship as collaborators is the source of their success working together. According to Feld (in the same Dunning article), "I feel that she looks at each ballet and tries to understand its nature, and then tries to invent material to reveal that nature. She's not stuck in a style. She tries to reinvent each time."

Endsong, a piece based on Richard Strauss' *Four Last Songs*, had its world premiere on September 27, 1991, at Alverno College's Pitman Theatre in Milwaukee, Wisconsin. (The work was actually danced in silence because of a dispute over licensing with the Strauss estate.) *Evoe* and *Clave* (a solo piece danced by Buffy Miller) had their world debuts at Milwaukee's Pabst Theatre on the same day.

The year 1991 had been a busy year, and 1992 would prove to be much the same. She would design more ballets for Eliot Feld, create costumes for a new play by John Guare, and return as a designer for opera, one of her life-long passions. But the year would begin with work with some old friends on a new adaptation of a classic ballet.

Jane Hermann was a long-time colleague and good friend of Willa Kim. They had first met in 1963 at the Joffrey Ballet, where Miss Hermann worked in audience development and as an assistant general manager. Hermann went on to work as co-administrator (with Cora Cahan) of the Feld Ballet before becoming director of presentations at the Metropolitan Opera House in 1976. In 1989 Miss Hermann succeeded Charles Dillingham as Executive Director of the American Ballet Theatre (ABT), and in 1990 she became co-director of ABT with Oliver Smith.

It was Hermann's idea to update and return Serge Prokofiev's classic, *Peter and the Wolf*, to the ABT repertory. The hour-long ballet was originally choreographed by Adolph Bohm in 1940 as a children's ballet for the company then known as Ballet Theatre. Despite some initial reluctance to do a ballet that would mainly be performed at matinees for children, Michael Smuin agreed to choreograph the new version, with a libretto written by film and television writer Larry Gelbart. Smuin wanted Willa Kim to design the costumes and Tony Walton to design the sets. Jane Hermann agreed and added lighting designer Natasha Katz to the visual design team.

The world premiere of the new production of *Peter and the Wolf* occurred on January 18, 1992, at the San Francisco Opera House. The ballet opened to mixed reviews in San Francisco, but when it made its New York premiere on April 20, 1992, the reception by audience and critics alike was overwhelmingly favorable. Anna Kisselgoff wrote in the *New York Times* (April 22, 1992) that "The entire production has an engaging overall tone, filled with the free spirit that Prokofiev suggests children should never lose. Willa Kim's animal costumes are gorgeous paeans to colored feathers and fur, and Tony Walton's Chagallesque cutout translucent Russian landscapes, under Natasha Katz's vibrant lighting, recall folk art, never a cartoon."

On the same night that *Peter and the Wolf* had its New York premiere, the Feld Ballets/New York performed the world premiere of *To the Naked Eye* at the Joyce Theatre. The ballet featured Darren Gibson and seven women (including Lynn Aaron, Geralyn DelCorso, and Elizabeth Parkinson) dancing to music by Igor Stravinsky. Willa Kim's costumes—thin stretchy garments carefully constructed to reveal every movement were meticulously painted in shades of gray and black to divulge character and mood.

Mounting a new production of Giacomo Puccini's opera, *Tosca*, is a major investment for an opera company. In 1992 the Lyric Opera of Chicago and San Francisco Opera joined forces to mount a new *Tosca* which opened on September 11, 1992, at the War Memorial Opera House and was part of the San Francisco Opera repertory for the 1992-1993 season. Tony Award-winning director Frank Galati directed and Maria Guleghina made her San Francisco Opera debut in the leading role. *Tosca* opened in Chicago at the Lyric Opera House the following season on October 24, 1993 with Elizabeth Byrne singing the leading role. For Miss Kim, the opportunity to design for opera once again was welcome, particularly since Galati took a Brechtian approach to the production.

Shortly after *Tosca* opened in San Francisco, Willa Kim and Tony Walton returned to New York to design again for Tommy Tune. They were reunited with director Jeff Calhoun and lighting designer Jules Fisher, who brought along his co-designer, Peggy Eisenhauer. Tune was essentially creating a memoir of his life thus far, rendered in song-and-dance form. The ninety-minute review would stretch from his childhood days in Houston—when his desire to be a ballet dancer was overwhelmed by his towering height—to his successes on Broadway, with tributes to those who mentored and inspired him along the way.

Tommy Tune Tonite! A Song and Dance Act opened on December 28, 1992, at the George Gershwin Theatre. Tommy Tune was joined on stage by only two other dancers, Robert Fowler and Frantz G. Hall. The show, which had scheduled only a limited run in New York, embarked on a nationwide tour not long after its premiere. Soon it seemed that the tall, energetic Mr. Tune was everywhere, for *The Will Rogers Follies* was also beginning to be produced in theatres across America. Tune's success with both these shows was summarized by Stephen Holden in his December 29, 1992, review of *Tommy Tune Tonite!* in the *New York Times*. Holden wrote "As he taps his way across the stage of the Gershwin in diamond-studded shoes, the notion that you can tap your troubles away seems briefly to be more than just a quaint show-business conceit. Here is someone doing just that, right here and now."

The joy and exuberance inherent in a Tommy Tune production was a wonderful way to end the year. The new one, however, would bring sadness and loss. On February 4, 1993, Willa Kim's husband, William Pène du Bois, died in Nice, France, as the result of a stroke. His whimsical illustrations, his children's books, and his role as a founder of the *Paris Review* are an enduring legacy, and a testimony to his great creative spirit. The "William Pène du Bois Papers" form one of the special collections in the Manuscripts and Archives Division of the New York Public Library, where they were deposited in 1996 by his widow, Willa Kim.

After Billy's death, Willa Kim's work became even more the center of her life—if such a thing was possible. Two new Eliot Feld ballets had their premieres in early March. *Hadji*, a solo choreographed for Lynn Aaron, debuted on March 2, 1993, and *Frets and Women*, danced to music by Lou Harrison, were first performed on March 3, 1993. These ballets were part of the Feld Ballets/New York spring season and were performed along with several other dances from the repertory (many with costumes by Miss Kim), including *Clave*, *Evoe*, and *The Jig Is Up*.

What followed in early spring 1993 was a series of commissioned costume designs for a group of dance companies that were adding pieces originally designed by Miss Kim to their repertories. So intertwined was the original choreography with Miss Kim's original costume designs that they accompanied each other.

One such piece was *A Song for Dead Warriors* (1979), with choreography by Michael Smuin and sets and costumes by Willa Kim. The Dance Theatre of Harlem had begun performing it in 1984, but the work had not been a regular part of the company's repertory. The company revived it beginning on March 16, 1993, with a performance at the New York State Theatre at Lincoln Center. Early the following year, the Cleveland Ballet added *Stravinsky Piano Pieces* to its catalog of dances with a performance on February 9, 1994. *Stravinsky Piano Pieces* had been choreographed by Michael Smuin in 1982 for a performance at the White House. Ballet Florida began performing *Stravinsky Piano Pieces* on January 26, 1996, at the Kravis Center for the Performing Arts in West Palm Beach, Florida.

Hearts was another popular ballet designed by Miss Kim. It had its premiere on April 1, 1986, for the San Francisco Ballet, with choreography by Michael Smuin. Hartford Ballet Company added *Hearts* to its repertoire on April 29, 1994, with a performance at the Bushnell Theatre in Hartford. The ballet had also been done, beginning on May 5, 1988, by the Washington Ballet at the Kennedy Center.

One of her favorite pieces for Eliot Feld, *Doo Dah Day (no possum, no sop, no taters)*, opened on February 15, 1994, at the Joyce Theatre. It was performed by fourteen members of his company to a series of songs by Stephen Foster, including *Beautiful Dreamer, The Voice of Bygone Days*, and *Hard Times Come Again No More*. *Aurora I* and *Aurora II*, which had their debuts on October 16, 1985, were revived, as was *Skara Brae* from October 11, 1986. *Skara Brae* was danced to music from Scotland, Ireland, and Brittany.

Included as a premiere in that same season was *Doghead & Godcatchers*, which had its debut on March 2, 1994. Eliot Feld himself appeared in *Doghead & Godcatchers*, danced to Haydn's Symphony No. 60, "Il Distratto." He performed with his customary wit, and was accompanied by a large cast, including students from his New Ballet School. These students began the ballet learning steps from their teacher. Toward the middle, however, Feld was joined on stage not by students, but "as costumed by Willa Kim, the spirits who troubled him, including dancers portraying a giant caterpillar, a poodle, an eagle, a satyr, some sheep, and a goddess on a bicycle with enormous wheels," according to Jack Anderson in the *New York Times* (March 5, 1994). The entire ballet was pun—a play on words and on movement.

These dance debuts were in between the out-of-town and Broadway openings of *Grease*. The pre-Broadway tryout of this revival production of *Grease* opened at the Shubert Theatre in Boston on January 23, 1994, where the critics and audiences praised the parody-based interpretation of the popular musical. Set at Rydell High School in 1957, *Grease* was written by Jim Jacobs and Warren Casey, and directed and choreographed by Jeff Calhoun. Tommy Tune, who provided the momentum for the production, was credited as "Production Supervisor." Kevin Kelly, writing for *The Boston Globe* on January 24, 1994, lauded the costumes by Miss Kim, the scenery by John Arnone, and the show-stealing performance by Billy Porter as Teen Angel. Kelly predicted success in New York when the show opened on May 11, 1994, at the Eugene O'Neill Theatre.

Before arriving in New York, however, the show was on tour in Wilmington, Delaware, Washington, D.C. and Costa Mesa, California. The show featured celebrity-performer Rosie O'Donnell as Betty Rizzo, who benefited from the extensive number of preview performances as she honed her skills and became a valued member of the cast. The New York reviews were less positive than the ones out-of-town and bemoaned the production's lack of nostalgia for the 1950s. Miss Kim's costumes, however, were a success with the critics, with comments including "Willa Kim, who designed the costumes with shocking-pink heart-shaped bodices, is both a Broadway and ballet designer. She is on Mr. Tune's outlandish wave length." (NYT January 20, 1995).

The audiences, on the other hand, loved the show, which played for a total of 1,505 performances before closing on January 25, 1998. During the subsequent national tour, Miss Kim's costumes were seen in Cleveland, New Haven, Pasadena, Denver, and Toronto (among other cities) where *Grease* played to full houses.

Once *Grease* was running, Tommy Tune and his "team" (Willa Kim, Tony Walton, and Jeff Calhoun) went to work on another piece that Tune created, this time with lighting designer Richard Pilbrow. Based on the British tradition of street performers and set in pre-World War II London, *Stage Door Charley* (also known as *Busker Alley*) was a showcase for Tommy Tune's own considerable dancing skills. After opening on May 17, 1995, at the Temple Buell Theatre in Denver, the show went on tour. But it did not attract enough attention to warrant a Broadway opening.

Even as *Grease, Stage Door Charley*, and *The Will Rogers Follies* were touring throughout the United States, Miss Kim was busy in New York overseeing the construction of her costume designs for a new Broadway musical starring Julie Andrews. *Victor/Victoria*, directed and written by Blake Edwards, opened at the Marquis Theatre on October 25, 1995, after an out-of-town tryout stint in Minneapolis. The new musical featured music by Henry Mancini and choreography by Rob Marshall. Marshall and Kim both found inspiration in Brassaï's photographs of 1930s Paris, in particular for the look of "Chez Lui," the gay nightclub where the character Victoria Grant performs as Victor Grant.

The Broadway production was based on the 1982 movie musical with the same name that also starred Julie Andrews. Tony Roberts and Michael Nouri played the roles of Carroll Todd and King Marchan originally created by Robert Preston and James Garner respectively, but the spirit of the successful movie was translated to the stage—without the close-ups. Julie Andrews was triumphant in the role, wonderfully dressed by Willa Kim in both her female clothing as well as in her male-as-female drag costumes. Although Willa Kim retains the majority of her theatrical designs in her own possession, one of the original designs for the character Victoria Grant hangs in Julie Andrews' living room, commemorating Andrews' Tony Award-nominated performance.

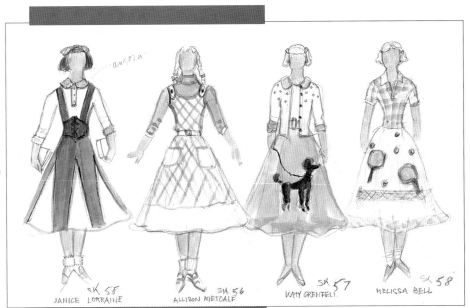

Grease

Costume Rendering by Willa Kim
for Janice Lorraine (SK#55),
Allison Metcalf (SK#56), Katy
Grenfell (SK# 57), and Melissa
Bell (SK# 58), 1994. Courtesy
of Willa Kim.

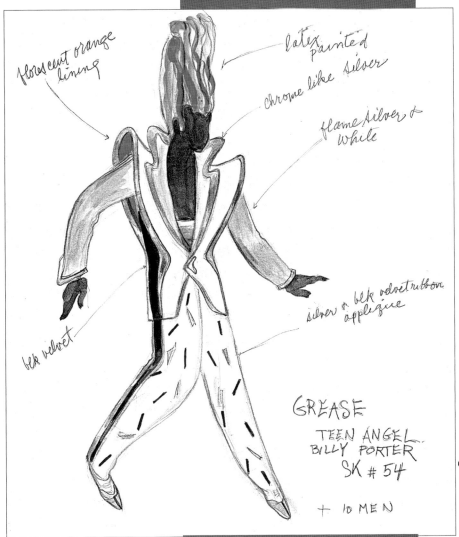

Grease

Costume Rendering by Willa
Kim for Billy Porter as "Teen
Angel," 1994. Courtesy of
Willa Kim.

In the spring of 1996, Miss Kim designed another new Eliot Feld ballet, *Paper Tiger*, set to music by Leon Redbone. It opened on March 1, 1996. In his review in the July 1996 issue of *Dance Magazine*, critic Gus Solomons jr proclaimed that the combination of Feld, Redbone, and Kim was an inspired one: "The gravel-voiced singer stretches a canvas of bluesy popular song, on which Feld doodles with fifteen picaresque characters, togged out in Willa Kim's fabulously motley wardrobe: Dickens by way of Threepenny Opera. Loose-jointed gamines in wacky hats and midi skirts sashay; bereted chaps in overalls cartwheel; everybody saunters in syncopation, like a New Orleans jazz funeral promenade."

Just prior to that premiere, Miss Kim had contributed costume designs to a revival of José Limón's 1966 ballet *The Winged*, as performed by the Julliard Dance Ensemble. It opened on February 15, 1996, in the Julliard Theatre. Soon afterwards she designed costumes for *Sunset Salome* by Peter Wing Healey (who wrote the libretto) and Max Kinberg (who provided the music for the production by the Mesopotamian Opera Company). The opera, starring Rochelle Mancini, Rebecca Wilshire, and Joe Gateley opened on April 8, 1996, at the Here Theatre, off-off Broadway.

The year 1996 also saw Miss Kim's return to designing costumes for figure staking, with designs for Japanese medalist Yuka Sato. After winning the 1994 World Championships in Japan that year, Tokyo-native Sato joined the professional ice skating ranks. Since then she has won numerous awards for professional competitions and toured extensively. Following an event she won in 1996, she was asked by a television commentator about the costume she was wearing, which seemed to express her movement so effectively. Yuka Sato explained that it had been designed "by the wonderful Willa Kim."

After her success with the costumes for Yuka Sato's, Miss Kim returned to her favorite medium: dance. The spring 1997 season for the Feld Ballet (renamed Ballet Tech just before the opening of the new season) included several new pieces for which she provided the costumes: *Juke Box*, which premiered on March 4, 1997; *Re: X* and *Evening Chant*, each of which debuted on March 7, 1997; and *Industry*, which opened on March 12, 1997. Often *Juke Box*—performed to music by Jerry Leiber and Mike Stoller as recorded by the Coasters—was paired with the powerful solo for Buffy Miller, *Industry*, as an effective contrast. *Industry* was choreographed to experimental music of the same name composed by Michael Gordon. During the season, Gordon and his group, Bang on a Can Live, often accompanied the dancers of *Industry*.

For *Industry*, Willa Kim designed a black unitard, with velvet surface texture for Miss Miller that had one leg made from the same material as the body of the garment. The other leg was covered in transparent black fabric that allowed her calf and thigh muscles to be seen. This was an especially effective design for a dancer whose fluid movements have made her a highly acclaimed performer. For the piece, Eliot Feld designed his own lights, which enhanced the angularity of the dancer's movement. For the first section of *Juke Box*, danced to "Little Egypt," Miss Miller wore a black wig anchored by a headband festooned with an asp. The interplay of costume, music, and movement pleased both crowds and critics.

Barely a week after the premiere of *Industry* Willa Kim attended another opening night, where her costumes were part of the evening's entertainment. On March 19, 1997, Maria Irene Fornés' new opera, *Terra Incognita*, opened at the Intar Theatre, off-Broadway. The opera was co-authored by composer Roberto Sierra, and was sponsored by the Intar Hispanic American Arts Center and the Women's Project and Productions. Set in Palos, Spain, *Terra Incognita* tells a series of stories of oppression. It featured Jennifer Alagna, Candace Rodgers-O'Connor, Matthew Perri, Lawrence Craig, and John Muriello, who were accompanied by Stephen Gosling on the piano.

Terra Incognita was just one in a series of plays and operas by Maria Irene Fornés that Willa Kim had designed over the years. The first was *Promenade*, which opened on June 4, 1969, at the Promenade Theatre. The theatre was itself new, situated on the corner or 76th

Street and Broadway, and was named for the first production to occur on its premises. The musical, described variously as "Candide-like" and "Brecht-like" and starring Madeline Kahn, Alice Playten, and George S. Irving, was nothing short of a triumph. The critics were also unanimous in their praise for the designers, including Jules Fisher (lights), Rouben Ter-Arutunian (sets) and Willa Kim (costumes). Miss Kim's especially effective costumes were recognized with a Drama Desk Award.

Among the other collaborations between Miss Kim and Miss Fornés was *The Office*, which closed in previews at Henry Miller's Theatre. Miss Fornés' play, directed by Jerome Robbins, had begun performing for audiences on April 21, 1966. Fornés and Kim would also combine their talents for *Fefu and Her Friends* for the production which opened at Santa Fe Stages in New Mexico on June 15, 1999.

Summers are quiet in New York City when most of the audience goes on vacation, so many theatres, dance, and opera companies go dark for the season. Just as the Santa Fe Opera provides a summer opportunity for opera singers, and Jacob's Pillow and the American Dance Festival provide an outlet for dancers, so the Williamstown Theatre Festival provides a summer venue for theatre and film actors. These "summer places" also provide opportunities for designers. During so much of her busy career, Miss Kim was so busy preparing for both the fall dance season and the new Broadway season that it was impossible to be away for even a short time during the summer. However, in 1997 she had the opportunity to work with actor/director Roger Rees on a play by Jon Robin Baitz, *The Film Society*. The play, starring Cherry Jones, opened in the Nikos Stage in Williamstown, Massachusetts, on June 25, 1997. Miss Kim had such a good experience there and the costumes were so successful that she returned to design costumes for *Under the Blue Sky* by David Eldridge. That production, directed by John Erman, opened on June 12, 2002. The following year she designed Henrik Ibsen's *Enemy of the People* for director Gerald Freedman.

Before these return engagements in Williamston, however, Miss Kim designed a 1997 Independence Day extravaganza. The American Ballet Theatre performed a short summer season at the Metropolitan Opera House, and the season was set to close on July 4th. To mark the occasion, the company revived a work from its repertoire: Eliot Feld's *Variations on 'America.'* The Feld Ballet had debuted the work on March 7, 1977, at the City Center, with Mikhail Baryshnikov and Christine Sarry dancing to the music of Charles Ives and William Schuman. American Ballet Theatre had first performed the ballet (using Miss Kim's original costume designs) on January 9, 1982, with Mikhail Baryshnikov and Susan Jaffe in the featured roles. ABT's July 4th revival of *Variations on 'America'* featured Yan Chen and Angel Corella in the principal roles and used Miss Kim's original costume designs.

A life in the theatre requires lots of travel for out-of-town tryouts, production meetings, openings in a variety of venues, and occasionally for personal pleasure. From her first cross-country train trip in the mid-1940s to work with Raoul Pène du Bois, travels through Europe with her friend Margaret Stark and then her husband, William Pène du Bois, and visits with friends to Asia, Willa Kim has made many trips. She is a great traveler and will accept opportunities, especially if they involve travel to places she loves.

In 1982 she had taken the opportunity to travel to China. *Sayonara*, a musical based on James Michener's 1953 novel and the 1957 film adaptation starring Marlon Brando, was being considered as a potential production on Broadway. Miss Kim was approached about designing the costumes, but was not compelled by the story and was busy with other productions. When the producers suggested that she might need to take a trip to Japan to do research, she agreed. After traveling in China with friends, she stopped in Japan for three weeks to find some original sources for costumes suitable for *Sayonara*, but the production never materialized.

However, in 1998, she did in fact have an excellent reason to once again travel to Japan. This time the resulting costume designs were indeed constructed, worn for a very successful opening, and broadcast on television around the world. Miss Kim designed the costumes for Beethoven's *Ode to Joy*, performed as part of the opening ceremonies for the XVIII Winter Olympic Games. The event, which took place in the Minami Nagano Sports Park in Nagano, Japan, was broadcast in the United States on the CBS Television network on February 7, 1998.

With 50,000 spectators (including 2,500 athletes from 72 countries watching from inside the stadium), 80 ballet dancers danced to the concluding movement of Beethoven's Ninth Symphony. The twenty minute performance was choreographed by Gen Horiuchi (former principal dancer with the New York City Ballet and performer in *Song & Dance*) to live music conducted by Seiji Ozawa, who coordinated 2,000 singers from around the world using time-lag technology. The event was magical for all involved.

When Miss Kim returned to New York from her exhilarating experience in Nagano, she began a new collaboration with another choreographer, Ramón Oller. A native of Spain, Mr. Oller studied classical and contemporary dance in Barcelona, London, and Paris. An award-winning choreographer, in 1985 he created his own company, Metros Dansa Contemporania in Barcelona, and has since created many ballets for his own company and for others, including the Ballet de Cristina Hoyos and Ballet Hispanico.

Miss Kim had first designed costumes for Ramón Oller's *Bury Me Standing*, which the Ballet Hispanico premiered at the Joyce Theatre on December 1, 1998. The ballet is danced to traditional Gypsy melodies from eastern Europe and Spain. Later they worked together on *Eyes of the Soul*, which premiered on December 5, 2000. The work was set to music by the Spanish composer Joaquín Rodrigo as a celebration of a creative spirit's journey through life. The dance commemorated the 100th anniversary of Rodrigo's birth.

During the rehearsals for *Eyes of the Soul*, Oller returned to Spain to work with his Metros company, and was not available while the costumes were being made. Tina Ramirez, artistic director for Ballet Hispanico, completed the rehearsals and commended the final costumes as being perfect for the ballet—all without Oller's seeing them except for color copies faxed to Barcelona. When Ramón Oller returned to the United States he was enthusiastic about the costumes created by a designer that he obviously trusted.

The design team for *Eyes of the Soul* was the same one as for *Bury Me Standing*, with costume design by Willa Kim, set design by Eugene Lee, and lighting design by Roger Morgan. They would collaborate once more, on *Bésame*, danced to the "golden oldie" *Bésame Mucho* (*Kiss Me a Lot*). The piece was Miss Kim's third collaboration with Ramón Oller and the Ballet Hispanico. It opened on November 27, 2001, and was notable because most of Oller's previous ballets for the company were considered to be dark and moody. This one was considerably lighter and more playful, which extended to the designs created for the costumes by Miss Kim. Lighting designer Donald Holder created the lights for *Bésame*.

At the point in a career when people begin receiving career achievement awards, they are usually slowing down or even considering retiring. Not so Willa Kim. When she was awarded the 1999 TDF/Irene Sharaff Lifetime Achievement Award from the Theatre Development Fund, she was busy designing new ballets for Eliot Feld and Michael Smuin and new plays for Maria Irene Fornés and Gen LeRoy.

In 1993, the Theatre Development Fund presented a Lifetime Achievement Award to the legendary Broadway and Hollywood costume designer Irene Sharaff. After her death later that year, TDF renamed the award in honor of Miss Sharaff. Sally Ann Parsons of Parson-Meares Ltd., who had made so many of the costumes from Miss Kim's designs, presented the TDF/Irene Sharaff Lifetime Achievement Award to Willa Kim at the Marquis Marriott Hotel in New York City on March 2, 1999.

Less than a month later, Gen LeRoy's play, *Missing Footage*, had its world premiere at the Helen Hayes performing Arts Center in Nyack, New York on April 10, 1999. LeRoy's play was directed by her husband Tony Walton, and starred Tanya Gingrich, former principal dancer with the New York City Ballet, as a prima ballerina. Because Tony Walton was busy with the direction, the sets for *Missing Footage* were designed by Klara Zieglerova. *Missing Footage* was subsequently performed at the Old Globe Theatre using the same designs and much of the same cast. It opened in San Diego on July 24, 1999.

While in California for the opening of *Missing Footage* at the Old Globe, Miss Kim consulted with her old friend Michael Smuin, who was continuing to develop new ballets and revive old ones for his San Francisco-based company, Smuin Ballets. He planned to include a new version of the 1923 *Les Noces*, which Nijinsky choreographed to Stravinsky's composition of the same name, in his 1999 season. The ballet has a large cast and is full of colorful folkloric figures, with a Russian bride and groom at the center of the piece. Michael Smuin knew that Willa Kim would be an excellent designer for the updated version he had in mind. The Smuin Ballets version of *Les Noces* opened at the Cowell Theatre San Francisco on November 30, 1999, and remains in the company's repertory. After a performance at the Yerba Buena Center for the Arts, in San Francisco on May 3, 2000, Miss Kim's costume designs were nominated for the Bay Area's Isadora Duncan (Izzy) Dance Visual Design Award.

The ballets Miss Kim designed for Eliot Feld's Ballet Tech in 1999 included *Mending* which opened at the Joyce Theatre on April 27, 1999, created by Mr. Feld for Jassen Virolas and Patricia Tuthill. Miss Kim dressed the couple in thin, flesh-colored, stretchy fabric that revealed much movement, and made even the clothed parts of the bodies look if they were uncovered. Subtle areas of color and texture enhanced the eerie effect they created. Performed to music by Michael Gordon, the two dancers were separated, one in the air and the other on the ground, but gradually came closer and closer together. Eliot Feld, who was beginning to design as well as choreograph new pieces for his company, designed the set for *Mending*.

In the following year Miss Kim designed two more new ballets for Ballet Tech's spring season, *nodrog doggo*, which opened on March 21, 2000, and *Coup de Couperin*, which had its premiere on April 4, 2000. The unusual name of *nodrog doggo* refers to, and hides, the name of the composer of that particular ballet and many others for Feld, Peter Gordon. The music for *nodrog doggo* was Gordon's new composition, *I Buried Paul*.

For Feld's *Coup de Couperin*, performed to music by François Couperin and Marin Marais, Miss Kim designed costumes that echoed court-dancing in the eighteenth century. She used skeletal pannier hoops over colorful body stockings to depict the voluminous dresses worn by women of the time, and even put Spanish combs into the eight dancer's hair. The accompanying eight male dancers wore gray tunics that shimmered and tricorns on their heads. The impact was stunning, due to Miss Kim's use of what she often described as a "whiff of period."

Dancin' with Gershwin, with choreography by Michael Smuin and costumes by Willa Kim, had its world premiere at the Yerba Buena Center for the Arts in San Francisco on May 9, 2001. The New York premiere followed on August 13, 2001, at the Joyce Theatre, where the Smuin Ballet made a stop on the way to Prato, Italy, where they again performed the audience-pleasing ballet. The Gershwin music, songs and pieces for the orchestra are varied and memorable, and the piece fills an entire evening. From slinky gowns to frilly ones, the elements of costumes that were easily put on and taken off by the dancers added to the festivities. One of the high points of the ballet was Allison Jay's dance to Marilyn Monroe's version of "Do It Again" while wearing a tightly fitted, red velvet gown, with a very deep V-neck.

Miss Kim spent most of June commuting between her home on 82nd Street and Sag Harbor, New York, where she designed costumes for *Seascape* by Edward Albee. The Bay Street Theatre, a not-for-profit, 299-seat professional theatre in Sag Harbor sits on Long Wharf. It was founded in 1991 by Sybil Christopher, Stephen Hamilton, and Emma Walton,

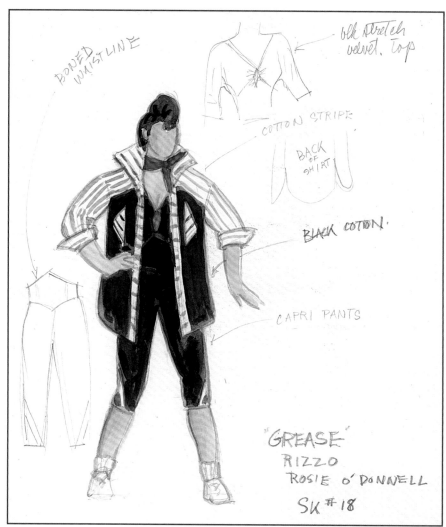

Grease
 Costume Rendering by Willa Kim for Rosie O'Donnell as "Rizzo," 1994. Courtesy of Willa Kim.

Grease
 Costume Rendering by Willa Kim for Jason Opshal as "Kenicke" in three scenes, 1994. Courtesy of Willa Kim.

Seascape
Costume Design for Susan Floyd and Ritchie Coster, 2001. Courtesy of Bay Street Theatre, Sag Harbor. Photo © Gary Mamay.

Seascape
Costume Design for Susan Floyd, 2001. Courtesy of Bay Street Theatre, Sag Harbor. Photo © Gary Mamay.

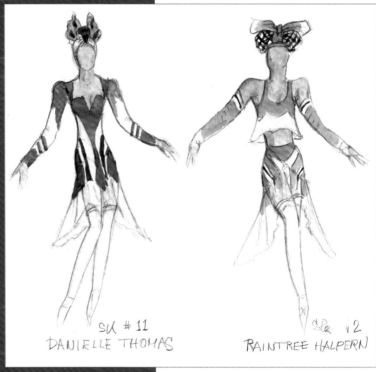

St. Louis Woman
Costume Rendering by Willa Kim for Donald Williams as "Biglow." Choreography by Michael Smuin for The Dance Theatre of Harlem. Courtesy of Willa Kim.

St. Louis Woman
Costume Rendering by Willa Kim for Danielle Thomas (sketch 11) and Raintree Halpern (sketch 12). Choreography by Michael Smuin for The Dance Theatre of Harlem. Courtesy of Willa Kim.

Rough Crossing
2004 Costume Design for Edward Hibbert and Richard Kind. Courtesy of Bay Street Theatre, Sag Harbor. Photo © David Rodgers.

Rough Crossing
2004 Costume Design for Christine Ebersole. Courtesy of Bay Street Theatre, Sag Harbor. Photo © David Rodgers.

Rough Crossing
2004 Costume Design for Tony Roberts and Christine Ebersole. Courtesy of Bay Street Theatre, Sag Harbor. Photo © David Rodgers.

and has produced several new plays and revivals that have been successfully transferred into New York City. The theatre is open from March through December, and the easy commute from Manhattan attracts performers and designers from the city. *Seascape*, starring Ritchie Coster, Susan Floyd, Josef Sommer, and Maria Tucci, and directed by Leonard Foglia, opened on June 19, 2001.

That same month Willa Kim received another lifetime achievement award, this time from the League of Professional Theatre Women. The not-for-profit organization was founded by Julia Miles in the early 1980s and has members not only from the New York area, but around the world, all of whom are active in the theatre. In 1998, The League of Professional Theatre Women created The Ruth Morley Designing Woman Award in honor of the film and theatrical designer, Ruth Morley (1926-1991). The first award was given to costume designer Jane Greenwood, the second to lighting designer Jennifer Tipton, and the third to Willa Kim, on June 7, 2001.

Miss Kim then designed a musical revue based on the life and career of Ethel Merman, *I Got Merman*. The production debuted on September 18, 2001, at the Stamford Center for the Arts, directed and choreographed by Tokyo native Amon Miyamoto, who co-wrote the revue with Dan W. Davis. *I Got Merman* was a huge hit in Japan, where it toured extensively before being brought to the United States. The American production featured three ac-tresses—Sandy Binion, Becca Ayers and Andi Hopkins—who portrayed Ethel Merman at various stages of her career. While Miss Kim's costumes for *I Got Merman* were praised by critics when it was produced in Stamford, the production failed to receive enough support for a Broadway run, though it has since been produced in a number of theatres.

The next season found Willa Kim designing for Christopher Durang's new musical play, *Adrift in Macao*, for which he also wrote the lyrics. It opened New York Stage & Film's 2002 season at the Powerhouse Theatre, on the Vassar College campus in Poughkeepsie, New York. Directed by Sheryl Kaller, the music had been composed by Richard Rodgers' grandson, Peter Rodgers Melnick. The musical is set in 1952 on the docks of Macao, China, and opens with the leading lady, Lureena, bemoaning her fate, having been abandoned by her companion. Her only remaining possession is the evening gown she is wearing. Before long, she is employed at the Surf and Turf Nightclub and surrounded by suitors and in-trigues. The musical was subsequently staged in New York for a group of potential backers, with the expectation of a 2005 opening off-Broadway, featuring much of the original cast and the original design team.

In the spring of 2003, Miss Kim returned to the Intar Theatre for her next designs. Abilio Estevez's *Havana under the Sea,* which pairs classic Cuban songs with an English language libretto, opened at the Intar on March 11, 2003. Miss Kim's costumes for the play's stars, Doreen Montalvo and Meme Solis, blended Cuban and Cuban-American ele-ments of color and design in the garments and their accessories. Willa Kim's old friend and colleague, Olive Wong, assisted in the production of *Havana under the Sea.*

On Monday, April 28, 2003, a celebration was held at Sardi's Restaurant, in the center of the theatre district, the site of many opening night parties. The occasion for this particu-lar event was the presentation of the Fashion Institute of Technology's 2003 Patricia Zipprodt Award for Innovative Costume Design to costume designer Willa Kim. The citation for the award, presented by her long-time collaborator, scene designer Tony Walton, recognized her talents as a costume designer in the worlds of dance, theatre, opera, and television. The evening's festivities included performances by some of the stars she had dressed: Cady Huffman (Ziegfeld's Favorite in *The Will Rogers Follies*), Anne Runolfsson (Julie Andrew's standby as Victoria Grant in *Victor/Victoria*), and Priscilla Baskerville (featured performer in *Sophisticated Ladies*). It also included tributes from other theatre and dance aficionados, including Betty Comden, who wrote the lyrics for *The Will Rogers Follies*, as well as *Wonder-ful Town* and *Bells Are Ringing* (on which Willa Kim assisted Raoul Pène du Bois).

Miss Kim did not pause long to savor the honor because she was busy completing the designs for two productions—a new ballet for the Dance Theatre of Harlem and *An Enemy of the People* at the Williamstown Theatre Festival, both planned for openings in the sum-mer.

The Dance Theatre of Harlem was scheduled to make its first-ever appearance in the Lincoln Center Festival at the State Theatre, beginning July 8, 2003. Early in 2002, Dance Theatre of Harlem's artistic director Arthur Mitchell approached Michael Smuin with the idea of creating an hour-long blues-ballet version of the 1946 Broadway musical *St. Louis Woman*. Smuin was delighted with the commission, especially after listening to the music composed by Harold Arlen with lyrics by Johnny Mercer. He was further pleased when Mitchell encouraged him to contact Tony Walton (sets), Willa Kim (costumes), and Jules Fisher and Peggy Eisenhauer (lights) to design the production. The team, who had last collaborated on *Peter and the Wolf*, was well-suited for the ballet version of *St. Louis Woman*, which was updated from 1898 to the 1940s.

The cast included three singers and forty dancers, who also sang. Miss Kim was able to provide a stunning distillation of the "Forties," avoiding long fussy skirts, which would have restricted the dancers' movements. She created flamboyant hats that incorporated

The Bay at Nice
Costume Rendering by Willa Kim for Estelle Parsons, as Valentina Nrovka, 2004. Hartford Stage, directed by Michael Wilson. Photo © T. Charles Erickson.

The Bay at Nice
Costume Design by Willa Kim for Estelle Parsons as Valentina Nrovka, 2004. Directed by Michael Wilson for Hartford Stage. Courtesy of Willa Kim.

Bury Me Standing
Costume Rendering by Willa Kim for Terry and Hector, 1998. Choreography by Ramón Oller for Ballet Hispanico. Courtesy of Willa Kim.

crystals, pearls
rhinestones on
silk net

crystals & pearls
on chassis

VICTOR
VICTORIA
JULIE ANDREWS
SK#12
FINALE

Victor/Victoria
Costume Rendering by Willa Kim for Julie Andrews as Victoria Grant,
Finale, 1995. Courtesy of Willa Kim.

African-based wrappings. Willa Kim's costumes combined with Tony Walton's brightly colored sets (inspired by the paintings of Romare Bearden and Henri Matisse) to create a colorful, exuberant hour of dance. *St. Louis Woman: A Blues Ballet* provided a triumph for the Dance Theatre of Harlem's debut at Lincoln Center.

After *St. Louis Woman*, Miss Kim herself was the subject of a production. The cable television station of the City University of New York airs public interest programs on Channel 75 in the New York area. CUNY TV launched a series of interviews with women working in the theatre, hosted by *Newsday* theatre critic and arts columnist Linda Winer. A total of thirteen interviews, *Women in Theatre*, created in cooperation with The League of Professional Theatre Women, were shown in the spring of 2003. The thirty minute program about Willa Kim was broadcast on June 13, 2003.

Willa Kim took a brief respite from the theatre early in 2004 to travel to Cambodia, Thailand, and Vietnam, but soon returned to her studio to design costumes for Christine Ebersole, who was starring with Dylan Baker, Edward Hibbert, Richard Kind, Gabriel Olds, and Tony Roberts in the Bay Street Theatre's production of *Rough Crossing* by Tom Stoppard. The production, directed by Daniel Gerroll, opened on June 15, 2004. Both Christine Ebersole and Tony Roberts were well clothed in casual and elegant summer apparel.

Shortly after *Rough Crossing* opened, Miss Kim was approached by Michael Wilson, artistic director at Hartford Stage, to design costumes for David Hare's play, *The Bay at Nice*. The cast included Estelle Parsons, who was featured in Willa Kim's first Broadway play, *Malcolm*, in 1966. Their reunion was a success, and also provided the opportunity for Richard Schurkamp to assist Miss Kim once again.

Soon afterwards she agreed to design costumes for *The Immigrant*, one of the productions to inaugurate the opening of a new off-Broadway theatre, Dodger Stages. Directed by Randal Myler, the play tells the story of the Harelik family, Russian emigrants who left Russia for rural Hamilton, Texas in 1909. Miss Kim's costumes effectively contrasted the dress of an eastern European Jewish family with the clothing worn by rural Texans in the early twentieth century.

In between taking the train from Penn Station to Hartford, Connecticut, and shopping in the Lower East Side for garments suitable for Russian emigrants, Willa Kim let a few messages pile up on her studio table. Once the two productions were open, *The Bay at Nice* on October 14, 2004 and *The Immigrant* on November 4th, she started to respond to the calls.

Mercedes Rhule and director Casey Childs had been wanting to discuss a series of costumes for a one-woman show based on the life of Peggy Guggenheim. Also a new production of *Turandot* was being planned for Santa Fe for the summer 2005 season, and the director Douglas Fitch wanted to look at the new Chinese art installation at the Metropolitan Museum of Art with her. Her agent had called several times about scheduling a meeting with Dirk Decloedt who was passing though New York on his way from California to his native Belgium and had an idea for a new Broadway musical. Christopher Durang wanted to provide some script changes to her before the backer's audition for *Adrift in Macao*, and wondered if she could find a beret for one of the actors to wear. The Joffrey Ballet was interested in the original designs for a revival of *Gamelan* for their 2006 season in Chicago. So many projects!

But, she always had wanted to do more opera. And so Willa Kim began to search her shelves of books and boxes of research for information about Chinese ranked dress, ornaments made from jade, and Asian mythology. She leafed through them and marked some interesting pages, and as she began to draw, new ideas evolved for her costume designs for the princess as a "whiff" of ancient China emerged, distilled from every production she'd ever done before, and from her own creative spirit.

Exhibits of Designs and Costumes

Art for the Stage
Touchstone Gallery, New York, NY
September 1975

Calder Celebration
Philadelphia Museum of Art, Philadelphia, PA
December 11, 1982 - February 6, 1983

Surrealism
Fashion Institute of Technology New York, NY
October 1, 1987 - January 23, 1988

Broadway: A Survey of Works by Scenic and Costume Designers
GImpel Weitzenhoffer Ltd & Howard Reed, New York, NY
September and October 1988

Salad Days
Fashion Institute of Technology, New York, NY
Summer 1993

Bloom: Fashion's Spring Gardens
Metropolitan Museum of Art, New York, NY
March 14, 1995 - July 5, 1995

"Fashion is a Verb!" F.I.T.'s 50th Anniversary Exhibition
Fashion Institute of Technology, New York, NY
February 14, 1995 - April 29, 1995

"Inside and Out: The Costumes of Barbara Matera, Ltd."
NY Public Library for the Performing Arts, New York, NY
October 21, 1996 - January 18, 1997

A Feast for the Eye: Food in Art
M.H. de Young Memorial Museum, Golden Gate Park, San Francisco, CA
September 26 - December 16, 1998

Salad Dressing: Food in Fashion
Copia: The American Center for Wine, Food & the Arts, Napa, CA
September 19, 2003 - January 12, 2004.

Designs and costumes in the permanent collections of the
* Fashion Institute of Technology, New York, NY
* New York Public Library for the Performing Arts, New York, NY

Willa Kim, 1981. Courtesy of Willa Kim. Photograph by Sam Siegeli.

Awards and Nominations

Emmy Awards
The Tempest (dance), 1981
A Song for Dead Warriors (dance), 1984

Obie Award
The Old Glory, 1964-1965

Drama Desk Awards
Promenade and Operation Sidewinder, 1969-1970
The Screens, 1971-1972

Maharam Award
The Screens, 1972

***Variety* New York Drama Critics Poll Award**
The Screens, 1971-1972

Tony Awards
Sophisticated Ladies, 1981
The Will Rogers Follies, 1991

Tony Award nominations:
Goodtime Charley, 1975
Dancin', 1978
Sophisticated Ladies, 1981
Song & Dance, 1986
Legs Diamond, 1989
The Will Rogers Follies, 1991

Asian Woman of Achievement Award, 1983
Asian American Professional Women

Irene Sharaff Lifetime Achievement Award, 1999
Theatre Development Fund, New York, NY

Ruth Morley Designing Woman of the Year Award, 2001
League of Professional Theatre Women, New York, NY

Isadora Duncan (Izzy) Dance Visual Design Award nomination, 2001
For *Les Noces*, choreography by Michael Smuin, for Smuin Ballets/San Francisco

Patricia Zipprodt Award for Innovative Costume Design, 2003
Fashion Institute of Technology, New York, NY

Distinguished Achievement in Costume Design, 2005
USITT (United States Institute for Theatre Technology)

Production Credits

The credits included here are for Willa Kim's major designs.

1961: June 12
Red Eye of Love (Play)
> Arnold Weinstein (Author)
> John Wulp (Director)
> Living Theatre, New York, NY

1962: January 3
Fortuna (Play)
> Arnold Weinstein (Author)
> John Wulp and Glen Tetley (Director)
> Maidman Theatre, New York, NY

1962: May 5
Birds of Sorrow (Dance / Premiere)
> Glen Tetley (Choreographer)
> Fashion Institute of Technology Auditorium, New York, NY

1963: March 10
Asylum or What the Gentlemen Are Up to Not to Mention the Ladies (Play)
> Gaynor Bradish (Director)
> Arthur Kopit (Author)
> Theatre deLys, New York, NY
> *Note:* Never opened.

1963: April 18
The Saving Grace (Play)
> Edward Harvey Blum (Author)
> Richard Altman (Director)
> Writers' Stage Theatre, New York, NY

1963: May 28
Birds of Sorrow (Dance / European Premiere)
> Glen Tetley (Choreographer)
> Netherlands Dance Theatre
> Théâtre des Nations, Paris, France

1963: October 25
Gamelan (Dance / World Premiere)
> Robert Joffrey (Choreographer)
> Joffrey Ballet
> Kirov Theatre, Leningrad, USSR

1963: November 3
Mark of Cain (Televised Dance)
> John Butler (Choreographer)
> New Dimensions in Television, WCBS-TV
> *Note:* Televised on "Lamp Unto My Feet."

1963: December 2
Have I Got a Girl for You
> (Broadway Play)
> Irving Cooper and Helen Cooper (Authors)
> Don Richardson (Director)
> Music Box Theatre, New York, NY

1964: January 14
Funnyhouse of a Negro (Play)
> Adrienne Kennedy (Author)
> Michael Kahn (Director)
> Theater 1964
> East End Theatre, New York, NY

1964: March 15
Dynamite Tonight! (Comic Opera)
> Arnold Weinstein (Author)
> William Bolcom (Music)
> Paul Sills, Arnold Weinstein, Mike Nichols, Lee Strasberg (Directors)
> Actors Studio Theatre
> York Playhouse, New York, NY
> *Note:* Also scenic design.

1964: June 26
A Midsummer Night's Dream (Play)
> William Shakespeare (Author)
> Jack Sydow (Director)
> New York Shakespeare Festival Mobile Theatre
> Mount Morris Park, New York, NY

1964: November 1
The Old Glory (Play)
> Robert Lowell (Author)
> Jonathan Miller (Director)
> American Place Theatre (Inaugural Production)
> St. Clement's Church, New York, NY
> *Note:* Obie Award.

1964: December 10
Helen (Play)
> Wallace Grey (Author)
> Michael Kahn (Director)
> Bouwerie Lane Theatre, New York, NY

1965: January 8
The Forced Marriage
(Televised Play)
Molière (Author)
David Susskind (Host)
The Esso Repertory Theatre
NET (National Educational Television)

1965: January 28
The Beautiful People
(Televised Play)
William Saroyan (Author)
David Susskind (Host)
The Esso Repertory Theatre
NET (National Educational Television)

1965: March 15
The Day the Whores Came Out to Play Tennis and *Sing to Me Through Open Windows* (Plays)
Arthur Kopit (Author)
Gerald Freeman (Director)
Players Theatre, New York, NY

1965: March 17
St. Patrick's Day (Televised Play)
Robert Sheridan (Author)
David Susskind (Host)
Michael Murray (Director)
The Esso Repertory Theatre
NET (National Educational Television)
Note: Performed by The Charles Playhouse, Boston, MA.

1965: July 1
The Game of Noah (Dance / World Premiere)
Glen Tetley (Choreographer)
Netherlands Dance Theatre
Holland Festival, The Hague, Netherlands

1965: August 6
The Stag King (Opera / American Premiere)
Hans Werner Henze (Composer)
Bliss Hebert (Director)
Santa Fe Opera Company, Santa Fe, NM

1965: August 11
The Game of Noah (Dance / American Premiere)
Glen Tetley (Choreographer)
Joffrey Ballet
Jacob's Pillow Dance Festival, Lee, MA
Note: Also scenic design.

1965: September 9
Gamelan (Dance / American Premiere)
Robert Joffrey (Choreographer)
Robert Joffrey Ballet
Delacorte Theatre, Central Park, New York, NY

1965: October 11
Benito Cereno (Televised Play)
Robert Lowell (Author)
American Place Theatre
NET (National Educational Television)

1966: January 11
Malcolm (Broadway Play)
Edward Albee (Author)
Alan Schneider (Director)
Shubert Theatre, New York, NY

1966: April 1
In Search of "Lovers" (Dance)
Glen Tetley (Choreographer)
New Rorem (Music)
Glen Tetley Company
Hunter College Playhouse, New York, NY
Note: Also scenic design.

1966: April 21
The Office (Broadway Play)
Maria Irene Fornés (Author)
Robert Prince (Music)
Jerome Robbins (Director)
Henry Miller's Theatre, New York, NY
Note: Closed in previews.

1966: May 3
In Search of "Lovers" (Televised Dance)
Glen Tetley (Choreographer)
New Dimensions in Television
Channel 13, WNET

1966: September 7
Nightwings (Dance / Premiere)
Gerald Arpino (Choreographer)
City Center Joffrey Ballet
City Center, New York, NY

1966: November 15
Chu Chem (Play / Pre-Broadway Tryout)
Mitch Leigh (Author)
Albert Marre (Director)
Locust Theatre, Philadelphia, PA
Note: Costume design with Howard Bay.

1966: November 28
Hail Scrawdyke! (Broadway Play)
David Halliwell (Author)
Alan Arkin (Director)
Booth Theatre, New York, NY

1967: July
Seven Deadly Sins (Dance / Premiere)
Glen Tetley (Choreographer)
Glen Tetley Dance Company
Queen Elizabeth Theatre, Vancouver, British Columbia, Canada
Note: Commissioned by Vancouver Symphony for the Vancouver Festival.

1967: October 10
Scuba Duba (Off-Broadway Play)
Bruce Jay Friedman (Author)
Jacques Levy (Director)
The New Theatre, New York, NY

1967: December 14
The Ceremony of Innocence (Play)
Ronald Ribman (Author)
Arthur A. Seidelman (Director)
American Place Theatre at St. Clement's, New York, NY

1968: August
The Magic Flute (Opera)
Bliss Hebert (Director)
Santa Fe Opera Company
Santa Fe, NM

Le Rossignol: Stravinsky Remembered
Costume Design by Willa Kim. Santa Fe Opera (1969) for National Educational
Television, 1971. Courtesy of Willa Kim.

1968: December 10
Brahms Quintet (Dance / Premiere)
 Dennis Nahat (Choreographer)
 American Ballet Theatre
 Brooklyn Academy of Music, Brooklyn, NY

1969: April 1
The Crucible (Play)
 Arthur Miller (Author)
 Curt Dempster (Director)
 Smith College, Northampton, MA
 Note: Dedication production for the
  Mendenhall Center for the Performing Arts.

1969: April 23
Papp (Play)
 Kenneth Cameron (Author)
 Martin Fried (Director)
 American Place Theatre
 St. Clement's Church, New York, NY

1969: June 4
Promenade (Musical)
 Maria Irene Fornés (Book and Lyrics)
 Al Carmines (Music)
 Lawrence Kornfeld (Director)
 Promenade Theatre, New York, NY
 Note: Drama Desk Award.

1969: July
Le Rossignol (Opera)
 Igor Stravinsky (Composer)
 Bliss Hebert (Director)
 Santa Fe Opera Company
 Santa Fe, NM
 Note: Also scenic design.

1969: August 1
Help! Help! The Globolinks
 (Opera / American Premiere)
 Gian Carlo Menotti (Composer & Librettist)
 Santa Fe Opera Company
 Santa Fe, NM
 Note: Also scenic design.

1969: October 8
*Two Evenings of Short Plays for the
New Theatre for Now* (Plays)
 Edward Parone (Director)
 Center Theatre Group
 Music Center, Mark Taper Forum,
  Los Angeles, CA

1969: October 9
*Two Evenings of Short Plays for the
New Theatre for Now* (Plays)
 Joel Schwartz (*Tilt* / Author and Director)
 Israel Horowitz (*Line* / Author)
 Gordon Davidson (*Line* / Director)
 Center Theatre Group
 Music Center, Mark Taper Forum,
  Los Angeles, CA

1969: December 22
Help! Help! The Globolinks (Opera)
 Gian Carlo Menotti (Composer and Librettist)
 City Center, New York, NY

1970: March 12
Operation Sidewinder (Broadway Play)
 Sam Shepard (Author)
 Michael Schultz (Director)
 Vivian Beaumont Theatre,
  New York, NY
 Note: Drama Desk Award.

1970: August
Jazz Theatre (Revue)
 Gordon Duffy (Author)
 Phoenix Theatre, New York, NY

1970: November 2
Sunday Dinner (Play)
 Joyce Carol Oates (Author)
 Curt Dempster (Director)
 American Place Theatre at St. Clement's,
  New York, NY

1970: November 10
Brahms Quintet (Dance)
 Dennis Nahat (Choreographer)
 Royal Swedish Ballet
 King's Theatre, Stockholm, Sweden

1970: November 29

Ontogeny (Dance / World Premiere)

Dennis Nahat (Choreographer)

Royal Swedish Ballet

King's Theatre, Stockholm, Sweden

1971: January 6

Ontogeny (Dance / American Premiere &
American Ballet Theatre Premiere)

Dennis Nahat (Choreographer)

American Ballet Theatre

City Center, New York, NY

Note: Also scenic design.

1971: October 27

Weewis (Dance / Premiere)

Margo Sappington (Choreographer)

Joffrey Ballet

City Center, New York, NY

1971: November 22

Le Rossignol: Stravinsky Remembered
(Televised Opera)

Igor Stravinsky (Composer)

Santa Fe Opera Company

NET (National Educational Television)

Note: Also scenic design.

1971: November 30

The Screens (Play / American Premiere)

Jean Genet (Author)

Minos Volanakis (Director)

Chelsea Theatre Center (Company)

Brooklyn Academy of Music,
    Brooklyn, NY

Note: Drama Desk Award, *Variety* New
    York Drama Critics Poll Award, and
    Maharam Award.

1972: January 24

Tragic Celebration (Hara-Kiri)
(Dance / Premiere)

John Butler and Lawrence Rhodes
    (Choreographers)

City Center, New York, NY

1972: February 22

Sleep (Play)

Jack Gelber (Author)

Jacque Levy (Director)

American Place Theatre, New York, NY

1972: May 27

The Chickencoop Chinaman (Play)

Frank Chin (Author)

Jack Gelber (Director)

American Place Theatre, New York, NY

1972: November 13

Lysistrata (Broadway Play)

Aristophanes (Author)

Michael Cacoyannis (Director and Adapter)

Peter Link (Music)

Brooks Atkinson Theatre, New York, NY

1973: February 21

Jive (Dance / Premiere)

Eliot Feld (Choreographer)

Joffrey Ballet

City Center, New York, NY

Note: First ballet designed for Eliot Feld.

1973: March 22

Parade (Dance)

Léonide Massine (Choreographer)

Erik Satie (Music)

Jean Cocteau (Librettist)

Pablo Picasso (Costume and Set Design)

Joffrey Ballet

City Center, New York, NY

Note: Supervised reconstruction of
    Picasso's 1917 costume designs.

1973: October 12

Remembrances (Dance / Premiere)

Robert Joffrey (Choreographer)

Joffrey Ballet

City Center, New York, NY

1973: November

The Consort (Dance)

Eliot Feld (Choreographer)

Royal Swedish Ballet

King's Theatre, Stockholm, Sweden

Note: Also scenic design.

1974: February 18

Jumpers (Play / American Premiere)

Tom Stoppard (Author)

Peter Wood (Director)

Kennedy Center for the Performing Arts,
    Washington, DC

1974: April 9

Ceremonials (Dance / Premiere)

Norman Walker (Choreographer)

Harkness Ballet

Harkness Theatre, New York, NY

1974: April 9

Landscape for Lovers (Dance / Premiere)

John Butler (Choreographer)

Harkness Ballet

Harkness Theatre, New York, NY

1974: April 17

Rodin, Mis En Vie (Dance / Premiere)

Margo Sappington (Choreographer)

Harkness Ballet

Harkness Theatre, New York, NY

Note: Also scenic design.

1974: April 22

Jumpers (Broadway Play)

Tom Stoppard (Author)

Peter Wood (Director)

Billy Rose Theatre, New York, NY

1974: August 15

Janet Lynn, Figure Skater (Dance on Ice)

Shipstads and Johnson Ice Follies 1974–
    1975 Season

1975: March 3

Goodtime Charley (Broadway Musical)

Sidney Michael (Author)

Larry Grossman and Hal Hackaday (Music)

Peter Hunt (Director)

Palace Theatre, New York, NY

Note: Tony Award nomination. Starring
    Joel Grey.

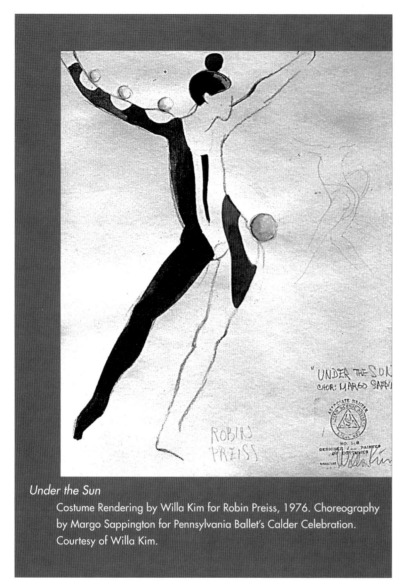

Under the Sun
Costume Rendering by Willa Kim for Robin Preiss, 1976. Choreography by Margo Sappington for Pennsylvania Ballet's Calder Celebration. Courtesy of Willa Kim.

1975: September 11
Death Is the Hunter (Dance / Premiere)
    Erick Hawkins (Choreographer)
    Erick Hawkins Dance Company
    Carnegie Hall, New York, NY

1976: January 1
City Center Joffrey Ballet (Televised Dance)
    Robert Joffrey, etc. (Choreographers)
    Joffrey Ballet
    Dance in America on PBS (Public
        Broadcasting Service)
    Note: Exerpts from Joffrey Ballet
        Repertory, including *Remembrances*.

1976: January 19
Remembrances (Televised Dance)
    Robert Joffrey (Choreographer)
    Joffrey Ballet
    Dance in America on PBS (Public
        Broadcasting Service)

1976: February 1
Face Dancrs (Dance / Premiere)
    Margo Sappington (Choreographer)
    Joffrey Ballet
    City Center, New York, NY

1976: April 9
The Old Glory (Play / Revival)
    Robert Lowell (Author)
    Brian Murray and Austin Pendleton
        (Directors)
    American Place Theatre, New York, NY

1976: October 7
Tactics (Dance / Premiere)
    Margo Sappington (Choreographer)
    Joffrey Ballet
    City Center, New York, NY

1976: October 7
Under the Sun (Dance / Premiere)
    Margo Sappington (Choreographer)
    Pennsylvania Ballet
    Shubert Theatre, Philadelphia, PA
    Note: Calder Celebration.

1975: March 20
Shinjū (Dance / Premiere)
    Michael Smuin (Choreographer)
    San Francisco Ballet
    War Memorial Opera House, San Francisco, CA
    Note: Also scenic design. First ballet
        designed for Michael Smuin.

1975: May 17
Daphnis und Chloe (Dance / World Premiere)
    Glen Tetley (Choreographer)
    Stuttgart Ballet
    Wuerttemberg State Theatre, Stuttgart,
        Germany
    Note: Also scenic design.

1975: June 12
Daphnis and Chloe (Dance / American Premiere)
    Glen Tetley (Choreographer)
    Stuttgart Ballet
    Metropolitan Opera House, New York, NY
    Note: Also scenic design.

1975: July 22
Angelitos Negres (Televised Dance)
    Realidades Series, Latino Television
        Broadcasting Service
    Channel 13, WNET
    Note: Art Director.

1976: October 20

Impromptu (Dance / Premiere)

    Eliot Feld (Choreographer)

    The Feld Ballet

    Newman Theatre, New York, NY

1976: October 21

Orpheus Times Light Squared (Dance / Premiere)

    Gerald Arpino (Choreographer)

    Joffrey Ballet

    City Center, New York, NY

    Note: Also scenic design.

1977: March 7

Variations on 'America' (Dance / Premiere)

    Eliot Fold (Choroographor)

    The Feld Ballet

    City Center, New York, NY

1977: March 12

A Footstep of Air (Dance / Premiere)

    Eliot Feld (Choreographer)

    The Feld Ballet

    City Center, New York, NY

1977: June 4

Nocturne (Dance / Premiere)

    Glen Tetley (Choreographer)

    Gaillard Municipal Auditorium, Spoleto
        Festival U.S.A., Charleston, SC

    Note: Sriabin Gala.

1977: August 11

Santa Fe Saga (Dance / Premiere)

    Eliot Feld (Choreographer)

    The Feld Ballet

    ArtPark, Lewistown, NY

1977: December 9

Sphinx (Dance / Premiere)

    Glen Tetley (Choreographer)

    American Ballet Theatre

    Kennedy Center for the Performing Arts,
        Washington, DC

1978: March 27

Dancin' (Broadway Musical)

    Bob Fosse (Director and Choreographer)

    Gordon Lowry-Harrell (Music Arranger and
        Conductor)

    Broadhurst Theatre, New York, NY

    Note: Tony Award nomination.

1978: April 13

La Vida (Dance / Premiere)

    Eliot Feld (Choreographer)

    The Feld Ballet

    Plymouth Theatre, New York, NY

1978: May 9

Capriccio for Piano and Orchestra
(Dance / Premiere)

    Robert Gladstein (Choreographer)

    San Francisco Ballet

    War Memorial Opera House, San Francisco, CA

1978: August 1

Sphinx (Dance)

    Glen Tetley (Choreographer)

    London Festival Ballet Company

    London Festival Dance, London, UK

1978: August 10

Danzon Cubano (Dance / Premiere)

    Eliot Feld (Choreographer)

    The Feld Ballet

    Wolf Trap Farm Park, Filene Center, Vienna, VA

1978: September 20

Half Time (Dance / Premiere)

    Eliot Feld (Choreographer)

    The Feld Ballet

    Newman Theatre, New York, NY

1978: October 12

The Grinding Machine (Play)

    Annalita Marsili Alexander (Author)

    Frederick Rolf (Director)

    American Place Theatre, New York, NY

1978: December 1

Medusa (Dance)

    Margo Sappington (Choreographer)

    Alvin Ailey Company

    City Center, New York, NY

1979: January 22

Contredances (Dance / Premiere)

    Glen Tetley (Choreographer)

    American Ballet Theatre

    Dorothy Chandler Pavilion,
        Los Angeles, CA

1979: February 23

Bosoms and Neglect (Play / Premiere)

    John Guare (Author)

    Mel Shapiro (Director)

    Goodman Theatre, Chicago, IL

1979: May 3

Bosoms and Neglect (Broadway Play)

    Mel Shapiro (Director)

    Longacre Theatre, New York, NY

1979: May 16

The Feld Ballet (Televised Dance)

    Eliot Feld (Choreographer)

    Feld Ballet

    Dance in America on PBS (Public
        Broadcasting Service)

    Note: Excerpts from The Feld Ballet
        Repertory including *La Vida, Danzon
        Cubano.*

1979: May 17

A Song for Dead Warriors (Dance)

    Michael Smuin (Choreographer)

    San Francisco Ballet

    War Memorial Opera House, San Francisco, CA

    Note: Also scenic design.

1979: August 9

Papillon (Dance / Premiere)

    Eliot Feld (Choreographer)

    The Feld Ballet

    Artpark, Lewistown, NY

    Note: Also scenic design.

1979: December 7

Dream Dances (Dance / Premiere)

    Jirí Kylián (Choreographer)

    Netherlands Dance Theatre

    The Hague, Netherlands

1980: May 12

The Tempest (Dance)
> Michael Smuin (Choreographer)
> San Francisco Ballet
> War Memorial Opera House, San Francisco, CA

1980: May 29

Circa (Dance / Premiere)
> Eliot Feld (Choreographer)
> The Feld Ballet
> Eastman Theatre, Rochester, NY

1980: August 8

Scenes (Dance / Premiere)
> Eliot Feld (Choreographer)
> The Feld Ballet
> Performing Arts Center at SUNY, Purchase, NY
> *Note*: Also scenic design. Originally titled
> *Scenes for the Theatre* (1980);
> changed to *Scenes* (1982).

1981: January 18

Sphinx (Dance)
> Glen Tetley (Choreographer)
> Ater Balletó
> Teatro Municipale Romolo Valli, Reggio
> Emilia, Italy

1981: January 20

Brahms Quintet (Dance)
> Dennis Nahat (Choreographer)
> Cleveland Ballet Company
> Brooklyn Academy of Music, Brooklyn, NY

1981: March 1

Sophisticated Ladies (Broadway Musical)
> Donald McKayle (Book)
> Duke Ellington (Music)
> Donald McKayle and Michael Smuin
> (Directors)
> Lunt-Fontanne Theatre, New York, NY
> *Note*: Tony Award.

1981: April 5

The Tempest (Televised Dance)
> Michael Smuin (Choreographer)
> San Francisco Ballet
> Dance in America: "Live from the Opera House"
> on PBS (Public Broadcasting Service)
> *Note*: Emmy Award.

1981: April 28

Bouquet (Dance)
> Michael Smuin (Choreographer)
> San Francisco Ballet
> War Memorial Opera House, San Francisco, CA

1981: July 9

Dream Dances (Dance / American Premiere)
> Jirí Kylián (Choreographer)
> Netherlands Dance Theatre
> Metropolitan Opera House, New York, NY

1981: September 17

Daphnis et Chloe (Dance)
> Glen Tetley (Choreographer)
> Houston Ballet
> Jones Hall for the Performing Arts,
> Houston, TX

1981: October 1

Nomads (Dance)
> Jirí Kylián (Choreographer)
> Netherlands Dance Theatre
> Scheveningen, The Hague, Netherlands

1981: October 18

Family Devotions (Play)
> David Henry Hwang (Author)
> Robert Alan Ackerman (Director)
> New York Shakespeare Festival, New York, NY

1981: December 12

The Wild Boy (Dance / Premiere)
> Sir Kenneth MacMillan (Choreographer)
> American Ballet Theatre
> Kennedy Center for the Performing Arts,
> Washington, DC

1982: February 25

Lydie Breeze (Play)
> John Guare (Author)
> Louis Malle (Director)
> American Place Theatre, New York, NY

1982: April 6

Stravinsky Piano Pieces (Dance / Premiere)
> Michael Smuin (Choreographer)
> San Francisco Ballet
> War Memorial Opera House, San Francisco, CA

1982: June 3

Over the Pavement (Dance / Premiere)
> Eliot Feld (Choreographer)
> The Feld Ballet
> Joyce Theatre, New York, NY

1983: April 16

Summer's Lease (Dance / Premiere)
> Eliot Feld (Choreographer)
> The Feld Ballet
> Joyce Theatre, New York, NY

1983: April 20

Three Dances (Dance / Premiere)
> Eliot Feld (Choreographer)
> The Feld Ballet
> Joyce Theatre, New York, NY

1983: May 11

Sphinx (Dance)
> Glen Tetley (Choreographer)
> National Ballet of Canada
> O'Keefe Centre for the Performing Arts,
> Toronto, Canada

1983: August 12

Chaplin (Musical)
> Michael Smuin (Director)
> Anthony Newley and Stanley Ralph Ross
> (Book, Music and Lyrics)
> LA Civic Light Opera, Los Angeles, CA

1983: October 18

Dream Dances (Dance)
> Jirí Kylián (Choreographer)
> Joffrey Ballet
> City Center, New York, NY

1984: January 16

A Song for Dead Warriors
> (Televised Dance)
> Michael Smuin (Choreographer)
> Dance Theatre of Harlem
> Dance in America on PBS (Public
> Broadcasting Service)
> *Note*: Emmy Award.

1984: March 7
Cabal of Hypocrites (Play)
Mikhail Bulgakov (Author)
David Margulies (Director)
Actors Studio, New York, NY

1984: April 10
The Jig Is Up (Dance / Premiere)
Eliot Feld (Choreographer)
The Feld Ballet
Joyce Theatre, New York, NY

1984: April 14
Adieu (Dance / Premiere)
Eliot Feld (Choreographer)
The Feld Ballet
Joyce Theatre, New York, NY

1984: April 30
Real McCoy (Dance / Premiere)
Eliot Feld (Choreographer)
The Feld Ballet
Joyce Theatre, New York, NY

1984: May 17
Elizabeth and Essex (Play)
Michael Stewart (Author)
Sondra Lee (Director)
York Theatre Company
Church of the Heavenly Rest, New York, NY

1984: June 20
Jamboree (Dance)
Gerald Arpino (Choreographer)
Joffrey Ballet
Lila Cockrell Theatre, San Antonio, TX
Note: Costume designs are in the Dance
Collection of the New York Library for
the Performing Arts.

1984: July 26
Butterfly (Dance on Ice)
John Curry (Choreographer)
John Curry Skating Company
Metropolitan Opera House, New York, NY

1984: July 26
Moon Skate (Dance on Ice)
Eliot Feld (Choreographer)
John Curry Skating Company
Metropolitan Opera House, New York, NY

1984: July 26
Presto Barbaro (Dance on Ice)
John Curry (Choreographer)
Leonard Bernstein (Music)
John Curry Skating Company
Metropolitan Opera House, New York, NY

1984: October 11
Stravinsky Piano Pieces (Dance)
Michael Smuin (Choreographer)
Pacific Northwest Ballet
Seattle Opera House, Seattle, WA

1984: November 21
Odalisque (Dance / World Premiere)
Glen Tetley (Choreographer)
National Ballet of Canada School
O'Keefe Centre for the Performing Arts,
Toronto, Canada
Note: 25th Anniversary Celebration of
National Ballet of Canada School.

1984: December 31
Odalisque (Dance / American & American
Ballet Theatre Premiere)
Glen Tetley (Choreographer)
American Ballet Theatre
Kennedy Center for the Performing Arts,
Washington, DC

1985: February 5
Papillon (Dance)
Eliot Feld (Choreographer)
San Francisco Ballet
War Memorial Opera House, San Francisco, CA
Note: Also scenic design.

1985: March 19
Brahms-Haydn Variations (Dance)
Michael Smuin (Choreographer)
San Francisco Ballet
War Memorial Opera House, San Francisco, CA

1985: April 3
Against the Sky (Dance / Premiere)
Eliot Feld (Choreographer)
The Feld Ballet
Joyce Theatre, New York, NY

1985: August 8
Mishima (Dance on Ice / Premiere)
John Curry (Choreographer)
John Curry Skating Company
Kennedy Center for the Performing Arts,
Washington, DC

1985: August 8
Spartacus (Dance on Ice)
John Curry (Choreographer)
John Curry Skating Company
Kennedy Center for the Performing Arts,
Washington, DC

1985: September 18
Song & Dance (Broadway Musical)
Andrew Lloyd Webber (Author)
Richard Maltby, Jr. (Director)
Peter Martins (Choreographer)
Royale Theatre, New York, NY
Note: Tony Award nomination.

1985: October 10
Medium: Rare (Dance / Premiere)
Eliot Feld (Choreographer)
The Feld Ballet
Joyce Theatre, New York, NY

1985: October 16
Aurora I (Dance / Premiere)
Eliot Feld (Choreographer)
The Feld Ballet
Joyce Theatre, New York, NY

1985: October 16
Aurora II (Dance / Premiere)
Eliot Feld (Choreographer)
The Feld Ballet
Joyce Theatre, New York, NY

1986: April 1
Hearts (Dance / Premiere)
Michael Smuin (Choreographer)
San Francisco Ballet
War Memorial Opera House, San Francisco, CA

Papillon
Costume Design by Willa Kim for Gloria Brisbin and students of the New
Ballet School, 1979. Choreography by Eliot Feld for The Feld Ballet. Courtesy
of Willa Kim. Photo © Herbert Migdoll.

1986: April 28
Long Day's Journey into Night
(Broadway Play)
   Eugene O'Neill (Author)
   Jonathan Miller (Director)
   Broadhurst Theatre, New York, NY
   Note: Starring Jack Lemmon, Peter
     Gallagher and Kevin Spacey.

1986: September 20
Sentimental Reasons (Dance)
   Michael Smuin (Choreographer)
   Cynthia Gregory and Company: Celebration Tour
   Lehman Center, Lehman College,
     New York, NY

1986: October 7
Echo (Dance / Premiere)
   Eliot Feld (Choreographer)
   The Feld Ballet
   Joyce Theatre, New York, NY

1986: October 11
Skara Brae (Dance / Premiere)
   Eliot Feld (Choreographer)
   The Feld Ballet
   Joyce Theatre, New York, NY

1986: October 14
Bent Planes (Dance / Premiere)
   Eliot Feld (Choreographer)
   The Feld Ballet
   Joyce Theatre, New York, NY

1986: November 23
The Front Page (Broadway Play)
   Ben Hecht and Charles MacArthur (Authors)
   Jerry Zaks (Director)
   Vivian Beaumont Theatre, New York, NY

1987: March 4
Tarantella (Dance / Company Premiere)
   George Balanchine (Choreographer)
   The Feld Ballet
   Joyce Theatre, New York, NY
   Note: Choreographed originally for the New
     York City Ballet.

1987: March 5
A Time Exposure (Dance / Premiere)
   Carolyn Carlson (Choreographer)
   The Feld Ballet
   Joyce Theatre, New York, NY

1987: June 1
Gardens of Stone (Film)
   Francis Ford Coppola (Director and Producer)
   Note: Costumes designed with Judianna
     Makovsky. Starring James Caan.

1987: September
Rodin, Mis En Vie (Dance)
   Margo Sappington (Choreographer)
   Houston Ballet
   Brown Theatre, Wortham Center, Houston, TX

1987: September 28
A Dance for Two (Dance / Premiere)
   Eliot Feld (Choreographer)
   The Feld Ballet
   Joyce Theatre, New York, NY

1987: November 19
Echo (Dance / Canadian Premiere)
   Eliot Feld (Choreographer)
   Feld Ballets/NY
   Premiere Dance Theatre, Toronto, Canada
   Note: Featuring Karen Kain of the National
     Ballet of Canada.

1987: December 16
*Julie Andrews: The Sound of
Christmas* (Television Special)
   ABC Television Network

1988: February 27
Shadow's Breath (Dance / Premiere)
   Eliot Feld (Choreographer)
   The Feld Ballet
   Annenberg Center for the Arts,
     Philadelphia, PA
   Note: New York premiere: February 2,
     1989.

1988: April 30
Dream Dances (Dance)
   Jirí Kylián (Choreographer)
   Vienna State Opera, Vienna, Austria

1988: April 30
The Unanswered Question
(Dance / Premiere)
Eliot Feld (Choreographer)
New York City Ballet
New York State Theatre at Lincoln Center,
New York, NY

1988: May 1
Dream Dances (Dance)
Jirí Kylián (Choreographer)
Grand Theatre de Geneve

1988: May 5
Hearts (Dance)
Michael Smuin (Choreographer)
Washington Ballet
Kennedy Center for the Performing Arts,
Washington, DC

1988: July 13
Petipa Notwithstanding (Dance / Premiere)
Eliot Feld (Choreographer)
The Feld Ballet
Teatro ai Parchi, Nervi, Italy

1988: July 15
Kore (Dance / Premiere)
Eliot Feld (Choreographer)
The Feld Ballet
Teatro ai Parchi, Nervi, Italy
Note: New York premiere: February 4,
1989.

1988: October 27
Shinjū (Dance)
Michael Smuin (Choreographer)
Ballet Metropolitan
The Ohio Theatre, Columbus, OH

1988: December 26
Legs Diamond (Broadway Musical)
Peter Allen (Music and Lyrics)
Harvey Fierstein (Book)
Robert Alan Ackerman (Director)
Mark Hellinger Theatre, New York, NY
Note: Tony Award nomination. Some of the
Costume Designs are in the Billy Rose
Theatre Collection of the New York
Library for the Performing Arts.

1989: January 1
Regina Wine Vinegar Commercial
(Television Commercial)
Advertisement for RJR Nabisco Brands, Inc.
Note: Garments are in the permanent
collection of the Fashion Institute of
Technology, New York, NY.

1989: February 4
Love Song Waltzes (Dance / Premiere)
Eliot Feld (Choreographer)
The Feld Ballet
Joyce Theatre, New York, NY

1989: February 8
Asia (Dance / Premiere)
Eliot Feld (Choreographer)
The Feld Ballet
Joyce Theatre, New York, NY

1989: February 15
Daphnis et Chloe (Dance)
Glen Tetley (Choreographer)
National Ballet of Canada
O'Keefe Centre for the Performing Arts,
Toronto, Canada

1989: October 9
Excursions (Dance / Premiere)
Eliot Feld (Choreographer)
The Feld Ballet
Joyce Theatre, New York, NY

1989: November 8
Dream Dances (Dance)
(Canadian and Company Premieres)
Jirí Kylián (Choreographer)
National Ballet of Canada
O'Keefe Centre for the Performing Arts,
Toronto, Canada

1990: December 8
Club XII (Rap Musical)
Rob Hanning and Randy Weiner (Authors)
Patricia Birch (Director)
WestBeth Theatre Center,
New York, NY

1991: February 2
Ion (Dance / Premiere)
Eliot Feld (Choreographer)
Feld Ballets/NY
Joyce Theatre, New York, NY

1991: February 10
Fauna (Dance / Premiere)
Eliot Feld (Choreographer)
Feld Ballets/NY
Joyce Theatre, New York, NY

1991: May 1
The Will Rogers Follies (Broadway Musical)
Peter Stone (Book)
Betty Comden and Adolph Green (Lyricists)
Cy Coleman (Music)
Tommy Tune (Director and Choreographer)
Palace Theatre, New York, NY
Note: Tony Award.

1991: September 27
Endsong (Dance / Premiere)
Eliot Feld (Choreographer)
Feld Ballets/NY
Pitman Theatre, Alverno College, Milwaukee, WI

1991: September 28
Clave (Dance / Premiere)
Eliot Feld (Choreographer)
Feld Ballets/NY
Pabst Theatre, Milwaukee, WI

1991: September 28
Evoe (Dance / Premiere)
Eliot Feld (Choreographer)
Feld Ballets/NY
Pabst Theatre, Milwaukee, WI

1992: January 18
Peter and the Wolf (Dance / Premiere)
Michael Smuin (Choreographer)
American Ballet Theatre
San Francisco Opera House,
San Francisco, CA

St. Louis Woman
Costume Rendering by Willa Kim for Christiane Cristo (sketch 10).
Choreography by Michael Smuin for The Dance Theatre of Harlem.
Courtesy of Willa Kim.

1992: March 18
Four Baboons Adoring the Sun
(Broadway Play)
John Guare (Author)
Peter Hall (Director)
Vivian Beaumont Theatre, Lincoln Center,
New York, NY

1992: April 20
To the Naked Eye (Dance / Premiere)
Eliot Feld (Choreographer)
The Feld Ballet
Joyce Theatre, New York, NY

1992: September 11
Tosca (Opera)
Giacomo Puccini (Composer)
Frank Galati (Director)
Lyric Opera of Chicago / San Francisco
Opera co-production
War Memorial Opera House, San Francisco, CA

1992: December 28
*Tommy Tune Tonite! A Song and
Dance Act* (Broadway Musical)
George Gershwin Theatre,
New York, NY

1993: March 2
Hadji (Dance / Premiere)
Eliot Feld (Choreographer)
Feld Ballets/NY
Joyce Theatre, New York, NY

1993: March 3
Frets and Women (Dance / Premiere)
Eliot Feld (Choreographer)
Feld Ballets/NY
Joyce Theatre, New York, NY

1993: March 10
*With Dew upon Their Feet
(aka Blooms Wake)* (Dance / Premiere)
Eliot Feld (Choreographer)
Feld Ballets/NY
Joyce Theatre, New York, NY
Note: Renamed "With Dew Upon Their
Feet" in 1996. Also scenic design.

1993: March 16
A Song for Dead Warriors (Dance)
Michael Smuin (Choreographer)
Dance Theatre of Harlem
New York State Theatre at Lincoln Center,
New York, NY
Note: Also scenic design.

1993: March 25
Sphinx (Dance)
Glen Tetley (Choreographer)
Den Morske Masjonal Ballet
Den Morske Opera House, Oslo, Norway

1993: October 24
Tosca (Opera)
Giacomo Puccini (Composer)
Frank Galati (Director)
Lyric Opera of Chicago / San Francisco
Opera co-production
Lyric Opera House, Chicago, IL

1994: February 9
Stravinsky Piano Pieces (Dance)
Michael Smuin (Choreographer)
Cleveland Ballet Company

1994: February 14
23 Skidoo (Dance / Premiere)
Eliot Feld (Choreographer)
Kids Dance (Ballet Tech)
Joyce Theatre, New York, NY

1994: February 15
*Doo Dah Day (no possum, no sop, no
taters)* (Dance / Premiere)
Eliot Feld (Choreographer)
The Feld Ballet
Joyce Theatre, New York, NY

1994: March 2
Doghead & Godcatchers (Dance / Premiere)
Eliot Feld (Choreographer)
Feld Ballets/NY
Joyce Theatre, New York, NY

1994: April 29
Hearts (Dance)
Michael Smuin (Choreographer)
Hartford Ballet Company
Bushnell Theatre, Hartford, CT

1994: May 11
Grease (Broadway Musical)
Jim Jacobs and Warren Casey (Book, Music and Lyrics)
Jeff Calhoun (Director and Choreographer)
Tommy Tune (Production Supervisor)
Eugene O'Neill Theatre, New York, NY

1995: March 8
Chi (Dance / Premiere)
Eliot Feld (Choreographer)
Feld Ballets/NY
Joyce Theatre, New York, NY

1995: May 17
Stage Door Charley (aka Busker Alley) (Musical)
A.J. Carothers, Richard M. and Robert B. Sherman (Authors)
Jeff Calhoun (Director and Choreographer)
Temple Buell Theatre, Denver, CO
Note: Starring Tommy Tune.

1995: October 25
Victor/Victoria (Broadway Musical)
Blake Edwards (Book and Director)
Henry Mancini (Music)
Leslie Bricusse (Lyricist)
Rob Marshall (Choreographer)
Marquis Theatre, New York, NY
Note: Starring Julie Andrews.

1996:
Yuka Sato (Figure Skating)
Note: New York performance: September 29, 1996.

1996: January 26
Brahms-Haydn Variations (Dance)
Michael Smuin (Choreographer)
Ballet Florida
Kravis Center for the Performing Arts, West Palm Beach, FL

1996: January 26
Stravinsky Piano Pieces (Dance)
Michael Smuin (Choreographer)
Ballet Florida
Kravis Center for the Performing Arts, West Palm Beach, FL

1996: February 8
Bare to the Wall (Dance / Premiere)
Jacqulyn Buglisi and Donlin Foreman (Choreographers)
Buglisi/Foreman Dance
Pepsico Theatre at SUNY Purchase, NY

1996: February 15
The Winged (Dance)
José Limon (Choreographer)
Julliard Dance Ensemble
Julliard Theatre, New York, NY

1996: March 1
Paper Tiger (Dance / Premiere)
Eliot Feld (Choreographer)
Feld Ballets/NY
Joyce Theatre, New York, NY

1996: April 8
Sunset Salome (Musical Spectacle)
Peter Wing Healey (Librettist)
Max Kinberg (Music)
Lawrence Geddes (Director)
Mesopotamian Opera Company
Here Theatre, New York, NY

1996: May 23
The Tempest (Dance / Company Premiere)
Michael Smuin (Choreographer)
Milwaukee Ballet Company
Uihlein Hall at the Marcus Center for the Performing Arts, Milwaukee, WI

1996: November 21
Rodin, Mis En Vie (Dance)
Margo Sappington (Choreographer)
Théâtre du Capitole, Toulouse, France

1997: March 4
Juke Box (Dance / Premiere)
Eliot Feld (Choreographer)
Ballet Tech
Joyce Theatre, New York, NY

1997: March 7
Re: X (Dance / Premiere)
Eliot Feld (Choreographer)
Ballet Tech
Joyce Theatre, New York, NY

1997: March 8
Evening Chant (Dance / Premiere)
Eliot Feld (Choreographer)
Ballet Tech
Joyce Theatre, New York, NY

1997: March 12
Industry (Dance / Premiere)
Eliot Feld (Choreographer)
Ballet Tech
Joyce Theatre, New York, NY

1997: March 19
Terra Incognita (Play)
Maria Irene Fornés (Librettist and Director)
Roberto Sierra (Music)
Intar Hispanic American Arts Center
Intar Theatre, New York, NY
Note: Co-sponsored by the Women's Project and Productions.

1997: April 3
Under the Sun (Dance)
Margo Sappington (Choreographer)
Milwaukee Ballet Company
Uihlein Hall at the Marcus Center for the Performing Arts, Milwaukee, WI

1997: June 25
The Film Society (Play)
Jon Robin Baitz (Author)
Roger Rees (Director)
Williamstown Theatre Festival
Nikos Stage, Williamstown, MA

1997: July 4

Variations on 'America' (Dance)

Eliot Feld (Choreographer)
American Ballet Theatre
Metropolitan Opera House, New York, NY

1998: February 7

Ode to Joy (Dance)

Gen Horiuchi (Choreographer)
Minami Nagano Sports Park, Nagano, Japan
Note: Opening Ceremonies, the XVIII
Winter Olympic Games; broadcast in
the U.S. on CBS-TV.

1998: October 1

Rodin, Mis En Vie (Dance)

Margo Sappington (Choreographer)
LaGuardia High School of Music and Art and
Performing Arts, New York, NY
Note: Benefit concert.

1998: December 1

Bury Me Standing (Dance / Premiere)

Ramón Oller (Choreographer)
Ballet Hispanico
Joyce Theatre, New York, NY

1999: April 10

Missing Footage (Play)

Gen LeRoy (Author)
Tony Walton (Director)
Helen Hayes Performing Arts Center,Nyack, NY

1999: April 27

Mending (Dance / Premiere)

Eliot Feld (Choreographer)
Ballet Tech
Joyce Theatre, New York, NY

1999: June 15

Fefu and Her Friends (Play)

Maria Irene Fornés (Author and Director)
Santa Fe Stages
Santa Fe, NM

1999: July 24

Missing Footage (Play)

Gen LeRoy (Author)
Tony Walton (Director)
Old Globe Theatre, San Diego, CA

1999: October 19

Calling (Dance / Premiere)

Margo Sappington (Choreographer)
The Daring Project
Joyce Theatre, New York, NY

1999: November 3

Les Noces (Dance)

Michael Smuin (Choreographer)
Smuin Ballets
Cowell Theatre, San Francisco, CA

2000: March 12

In Paradisum (Dance / Premiere)

David Allan (Choreographer)
Orange County Performing Arts Center,
Los Angeles, CA
Note: Danced by Ethan Stiefel

2000: March 21

nodrog doggo (Dance / Premiere)

Eliot Feld (Choreographer)
Ballet Tech
Joyce Theatre, New York, NY

2000: April 4

Coup de Couperin (Dance / Premiere)

Eliot Feld (Choreographer)
Ballet Tech
Joyce Theatre, New York, NY

2000: May 3

Les Noces (Dance)

Michael Smuin (Choreographer)
Smuin Ballets
Yerba Buena Center for the Arts,
San Francisco, CA

2000: May 3

Shinjū (Dance)

Michael Smuin (Choreographer)
Smuin Ballets
Yerba Buena Center for the Arts,
San Francisco, CA

2000: May 3

Young Persons Guide to the Orchestra
(Dance)

Michael Smuin (Choreographer)
Smuin Ballets
Yerba Buena Center for the Arts,
San Francisco, CA

2000: June 1

Rodin, Mis En Vie (Dance)

Margo Sappington (Choreographer)
Carolina Ballet
Raleigh Memorial Auditorium, Raleigh, NC

2000: December 5

Eyes of the Soul (Dance / Premiere)

Ramón Oller (Choreographer)
Ballet Hispanico
Joyce Theatre, New York, NY

2001: May 1

Brahms Quintet (Dance)

Dennis Nahat (Choreographer)
Ballet San Jose
San Francisco Opera House,
San Francisco, CA

2001: May 9

Dancin' with Gershwin (Dance / Premiere)

Michael Smuin (Choreographer)
Smuin Ballets
Yerba Buena Center for the Arts,
San Francisco, CA

2001: June 19

Seascape (Play)

Edward Albee (Author)
Leonard Foglia (Director)
Bay Street Theatre
Sag Harbor, NY

2001: September 18

I Got Merman (Revue)

Dan W. Davis (Author)
Amon Miyamoto (Co-author, Director and
Choreographer)
Rich Forum, Stamford Center for the Arts,
Stamford, CT

2001: September 28
Sphinx (Dance)
>Glen Tetley (Choreographer)
>Dance Theatre of Harlem
>New York, NY

2001: November 27
Bésame (Dance / Premiere)
>Ramón Oller (Choreographer)
>Ballet Hispanico
>Joyce Theatre, New York, NY

2002: January 31
Sphinx (Dance)
>Glen Tetley (Choreographer)
>Marodni Divadlo, Prague, Czech Republic

2002: June 12
Rodin, Mis En Vie (Dance)
>Margo Sappington (Choreographer)
>Pennsylvania Ballet
>Merriam Theatre, Philadelphia, PA

2002: June 12
Under the Blue Sky (Play)
>David Eldridge (Author)
>John Erman (Director)
>Williamstown Theatre Festival
>Nikos Stage, Williamstown, MA

2002: Summer 12
Adrift in Macao (Play)
>Christopher Durang (Author and Lyricist)
>Peter Rodgers Melnick (Music)
>Sheryl Kaller (Director)
>New York Stage & Film
>Powerhouse Theatre, Vassar College,
>   Poughkeepsie, NY

2002: August 13
Our Town (Play)
>Thornton Wilder (Author)
>Jack Hofsiss (Director)
>Bay Street Theatre
>Sag Harbor, NY

2003: January 31
Sphinx (Dance)
>Glen Tetley (Choreographer)
>Ballet Florida
>Kravis Center for the Performing Arts, West
>   Palm Beach, FL

2003: February 28
Havana under the Sea (Revue)
>Abilio Estevez (Author)
>Caridad Svich (Translator and Adaptor)
>Max Ferra (Director)
>Intar Theatre, New York, NY

2003: April 3
The Tempest (Dance)
>Michael Smuin (Choreographer)
>Ballet San Jose
>San Jose Center for the Performing Arts,
>   Silicon Valley, CA

2003: July 8
St. Louis Woman (Dance)
>Michael Smuin (Choreographer)
>Dance Theatre of Harlem
>Lincoln Center Festival at State Theatre,
>   New York, NY

2003: August 20
An Enemy of the People (Play)
>Gerald Freedman (Director)
>Williamstown Theatre Festival
>Nikos Stage, Williamstown, MA

2004: June 15
Rough Crossing (Play)
>Daniel Gerroll (Director)
>Tom Stoppard (Author)
>Bay Street Theatre
>Sag Harbor, NY

2004: October 14
The Bay at Nice (Play / American Premiere)
>Michael Wilson (Director)
>David Hare (Author)
>Hartford Stage
>Hartford, CT

2004: November 4
The Immigrant (Musical)
>Mark Harelik (Book)
>Steven M. Alper (Music)
>Sarah Knapp (Lyricist)
>Randal Myler (Director)
>Dodger Stages
>New York, NY

2005: February 17
Woman Before a Glass (Play)
>Lanie Robertson (Author)
>Casey Childs (Director)
>Promenade Theatre, New York, NY
>*Note*: Starring Mercedes Ruehl.

2005: March 31
Shinjū (Dance)
>Michael Smuin (Choreographer)
>Ballet San Jose
>San Jose Center for the Performing Arts,
>   Silicon Valley, CA

2005: July 1
Turandot (Opera)
>Douglas Fitch (Director)
>Santa Fe Opera Company
>Santa Fe, NM

Operation Sidewinder
Costume Rendering by Willa Kim for "Apache #3," 1970. Courtesy of Willa Kim.

Index

This monograph on the career of Willa Kim is the first in what is projected to be an on-going series documenting the work of our best American theatrical designers. Theatre art is ephemeral, and nothing is more ephemeral than the work of the designers. After a production closes, only their sketches and drawings provide whatever record we have of the evolution of design in our theatre. The documentation of theatrical design in America, aside from a few books that document the work of notable American set designers, is fitful and sporadic. The USITT Monograph Series will, I hope, correct this. Our lives as theatre artists and scholars will be enriched by having available to us all the best of American theatrical design.

Del Unruh, Series Editor
USITT Designer Monograph Series
Lawrence, KS
January 2005

Bobbi Owen is Professor of Dramatic Art at The University of North Carolina at Chapel Hill. She has written four books and dozens of articles about theatrical designers and is active in USITT. She lives with her husband, Gordon Ferguson, in Chapel Hill, North Carolina.

the end